STERLING BIOGRAPHIES

CHIEF JOSEPH

The Voice for Peace

Lorraine Jean Hopping

STERLING

New York / London
www.sterlingpublishing.com/kids

To Marilyn for piquing interest, to Louise for teacherly advice, and to
Zachary for a kid's point of view

STERLING and the distinctive Sterling logo are registered trademarks of
Sterling Publishing Co., Inc.

Library of Congress Cataloging-in-Publication Data
Hopping, Lorraine Jean.
  Chief Joseph : the voice for peace / by Lorraine Hopping Egan.
    p. cm. — (Sterling biographies)
  Includes bibliographical references and index.
  ISBN 978-1-4027-6004-4 (pbk.) — ISBN 978-1-4027-6842-2 (hardcover) 1. Joseph, Nez Perce
chief, 1840–1904—Juvenile literature. 2. Nez Perce Indians—Biography—Juvenile literature.
3. Nez Perce Indians—Wars, 1877—Juvenile literature. I. Title.
  E99.N5J5835 2009
  971.00497'4124—dc22
  [B]
                                                                  2009024132

Lot #: 10 9 8 7 6 5 4 3 2 1
03/10

Published by Sterling Publishing Co., Inc.
387 Park Avenue South, New York, NY 10016
© 2010 by Lorraine Jean Hopping

Distributed in Canada by Sterling Publishing
c/o Canadian Manda Group, 165 Dufferin Street
Toronto, Ontario, Canada M6K 3H6
Distributed in the United Kingdom by GMC Distribution Services
Castle Place, 166 High Street, Lewes, East Sussex, England BN7 1XU
Distributed in Australia by Capricorn Link (Australia) Pty. Ltd.
P.O. Box 704, Windsor, NSW 2756, Australia

Printed in China

Sterling ISBN 978-1-4027-6004-4 (paperback)
          ISBN 978-1-4027-6842-2 (hardcover)

Image research by Larry Schwartz

For information about custom editions, special sales, premium and corporate
purchases, please contact Sterling Special Sales Department at 800-805-5489
or specialsales@sterlingpublishing.com.

Contents

INTRODUCTION: War or Peace? 1

CHAPTER 1: A Boy with a Heavy Load 2

CHAPTER 2: Speaking With Two Tongues 15

CHAPTER 3: A People Divided 25

CHAPTER 4: Young Chief Joseph 31

CHAPTER 5: Showing the Rifle 44

CHAPTER 6: The War of 1877 53

CHAPTER 7: On the Trail to Montana 64

CHAPTER 8: To Kill or Be Kind? 72

CHAPTER 9: Attack at Bear Paw 85

CHAPTER 10: Fame from Misfortune 96

CHAPTER 11: A Broken Heart 111

GLOSSARY 118

BIBLIOGRAPHY 118

SOURCE NOTES 119

IMAGE CREDITS 122

ABOUT THE AUTHOR 122

INDEX 123

Events in the Life of Chief Joseph

1840

Winter 1840
Joseph is born to Tu-eka-kas, chief of the Wallowa band of the Nee-mee-pu (Nez Perce).

November 29, 1847
Cayuse warriors murder thirteen settlers to avenge unjust treatment. The Spalding Mission at Lapwai, Idaho, is closed.

February 20, 1860
Gold is discovered on Nez Perce land near Clearwater, Idaho. Thousands of miners and other fortune seekers flood in.

1865
Joseph's daughter, Noise of Running Feet, is born. The U.S. Civil War ends, freeing soldiers to fight Indian wars in the West.

August 1871
Tu-eka-kas dies. Joseph becomes the band's civil chief. Frog is the war chief. That winter, homesteaders stake the first illegal claims on Joseph's land in the Wallowa River valley.

June 16, 1873
President Grant signs an order to split the Wallowa River valley, one half for settlers and the other half for Joseph's band.

May 14, 1877
General Oliver Howard orders all Nez Perce to move to the Lapwai Reservation within 30 days. To avoid war, the chiefs agree, except for Looking Glass.

June 17, 1877
War begins with the battle of White Bird Canyon. Warriors rout the soldiers, but the Nez Perce begin a long retreat to avoid further battles.

August 9, 1877
A surprise army attack at Big Hole, Montana, leaves the retreating Nez Perce with many dead and few possessions. Chief Lean Elk takes command and quickens the pace.

October 5, 1877
Chief White Bird escapes with about 170 followers. Chief Joseph surrenders. More than 400 Nez Perce are taken prisoner.

May 1878
Congress votes to move Chief Joseph's band to a reservation in Indian Territory (Oklahoma). Poor and ill-suited to the hot, dry climate, the band's number drops below 300.

May 1885
Prisoners who converted to Christianity are allowed to settle at Lapwai, Idaho. Joseph and about 150 followers move to the Colville Reservation in northern Washington.

1842
Joseph's brother Ollokut (Frog) is born. The boys spend winters at the Spalding Mission. The Oregon Trail opens the Northwest to wagon trains of settlers.

June 11, 1855
Nez Perce chiefs sign a treaty giving up land to white settlement in exchange for money, goods, and peace. Most of their land is off-limits to settlers, but the settlers quickly break the treaty.

June 1863
A year after the Homestead Act opens the West for settlement, Tu-eka-kas and other chiefs refuse a demand to give up 90 percent of their land. Christian Nez Perce sign the so-called thief treaty.

August 14, 1872
At council, Joseph demands that all settlers leave Wallowa. The settlers refuse. Agent John Monteith sends Joseph's appeal to Washington, D.C.

June 10, 1875
Grant takes back his order, opening Wallowa for settlement. Joseph struggles to keep the peace as conflicts between whites and warriors increase.

June 14, 1877
Against the wishes of Chief Joseph, warriors kill eighteen settlers to avenge a murder and many other injustices. Joseph's second wife, Springtime, gives birth to a daughter.

July 1, 1877
Soldiers destroy Chief Looking Glass's village and steal his horses. He joins the other chiefs and soon leads the retreat.

September 30, 1877
After evading troops for 1,500 miles, the Nez Perce are attacked at Bear Paw, Montana. Some escape to Canada; the rest hunker down in pits. Frog, Lean Elk, and other leaders are killed.

November 27, 1877
The prisoners arrive at Fort Leavenworth, Kansas. Dozens soon die of malaria and other diseases.

January 17, 1879
Chief Joseph meets with President Hayes to plea for aid and a return to Wallowa. His stirring words bring applause and fame but no action.

September 21, 1904
Chief Joseph dies.

1904

War or Peace?

If the white man wants to live in peace with the Indian, he can live in peace. There need be no trouble.

On a cold fall morning in 1877, a scout on a hill fired his rifle, waved his red blanket, and rode his horse in circles. The signal struck terror in the hundreds of Nez Perce camped below—for it meant, "Enemy attack, now!"

"Horses! Save the horses!" Chief Joseph cried. In a hail of gunfire from the charging soldiers, Chief Joseph and his twelve-year-old daughter, Noise of Running Feet, ran to the herd. They were too late. The uproar had split the herd and set the animals running, more than a thousand in number.

Joseph tossed his daughter a rope and told her to flee for her life. She lassoed a frightened horse and jumped on. Joseph watched her gallop away, black braids flying.

Bullets whizzed and pinged around him. Joseph mounted a horse and rode, unarmed, straight through a line of soldiers. He somehow reached his wife and infant daughter unhurt. His wife tossed him a rifle and cried, "Fight!"

Joseph never wanted to fight. He was a peace chief, a civil leader, who worked hard to avoid war. He truly believed his people and white people could live side by side in peace. Yet now the Nez Perce were under full attack from the U.S. Army. What started this war? What went wrong with Chief Joseph's quest for peace?

CHAPTER 1

A Boy with a Heavy Load

I have carried a heavy load on my back ever since I was a boy.

The boy who would become both famous and feared as Chief Joseph was born in 1840—the exact date unknown. If the season had been spring, summer, or fall, his birthplace would have been the cool, refreshing Wallowa River valley, the homeland of his people. High in the mountains of northeast Oregon, its rivers teemed with salmon. Rolling fields of tall, golden grass provided food for the prized horse herd, perhaps a couple thousand in number.

But Joseph was born in winter, when his people lived in the lower, warmer Imnaha River valley of Oregon. Each fall, the people strapped their children and blankets and

Each winter, the Wallowa men hunted game in the Imnaha River valley. As wildlife fled the busy campground, hunters had to travel much higher on the hillsides to find meat.

animal skins to horses and trekked along a narrow mountain trail. The path was so steep in places that the walkers found it hard to stand upright.

Several hundred people made up this Wallowa band, most of whom were related by blood. As **migrants**, they had no farms, no ranches, no plots of land for each family to call its own. Instead, they shared their mountain lands as a group. They lived easily and well off this land and off their horses and cattle. They traded with white settlers and other Native American people, offering fine-tuned bows and arrows and prized horses in exchange for hunting rifles, pots, tools, blankets, and other items.

Dozens of similar bands lived in the mountains and canyons of the Northwest, a region that would become the states of Oregon, Idaho, and Washington. These independent, roving bands shared a language, a lifestyle, a religion, and a name. They called themselves *Nee-mee-pu*, meaning, "The Real People." White settlers called them the Nez Perce.

Learning from Others

Why was a future Nez Perce chief named Joseph—a Biblical white man's name? In the New Testament of the Holy Bible, Joseph was the husband of the Virgin Mary, the mother of Jesus Christ.

The answer to this puzzling question begins in 1836. That year, Henry and Eliza Spalding set up the first Christian **mission** on Nez Perce land. The couple chose a site called

Henry Spalding, who set up a mission on Nez Perce land, translated the Gospel according to St. Matthew into the Nez Perce language. He printed the eight page booklet on the first printing press in Oregon.

Nee-mee-pu or Nez Perce?

Like most Native American people of the day, the Nee-mee-pu had no written language. Settlers, soldiers, and missionaries wrote down words and names as they heard them, using English letters to stand for Nee-mee-pu sounds. As a result, the spellings varied a lot. For example, what sounded like a *u* to one person might have sounded like an *o* to another. So as you read more about the Nee-mee-pu in other books, don't be surprised to see the name spelled many ways: *Nee-mee-poo*, *Nimipu*, or *Nimi'ipuu*, for instance.

As with many Native American groups, the Nee-mee-pu also took on a white-given name—Nez Perce. It means "pierced nose" in French. The French fur trappers who invented the name pronounced it "nez pair-SAY" and spelled it with an accent over the last *e*. However, the fashion of piercing the nose with shells belonged to a coastal people. The Nee-mee-pu were mountain people. It was an awkward case of mistaken identity that was never corrected.

English-speaking Americans who arrived after the French traders picked up this mismatched name. They pronounced it "nez purse," without the accent. In time, the Nee-mee-pu referred to themselves in the same way when they were talking to *so-ya-pu*—their name for white people. *So-ya-pu* means "crowned ones," because the Nez Perce were struck by the nineteenth-century fashion of wearing hats and bonnets.

This young Nez Perce man posed in 1910 in a traditional beaded necklace, moccasins, and fur blanket.

Lapwai (Place of the Butterflies) in northern Idaho, near the present-day Washington state border. As missionaries, their life's purpose—in the words of the day—was to "civilize the heathens." Above all, that meant converting "wild Indians" to Christianity.

Chief Tu-eka-kas, Joseph's father, welcomed the Spaldings. His purpose was to learn all he could from these strange newcomers to improve the lives of his people. This openness to other cultures had served the Nez Perce well. Through trading and travel, they eagerly adopted the skills and technology of others. From early pioneers to the northwest, they gained their first cattle. The Nez Perce soon bred these worn-out wagon beasts into strong, healthy herds. Thanks to the Shoshone, a Rocky Mountain group, the Nez Perce discovered horses. The Nez Perce learned to breed and train these useful animals so well that everyone prized their stock. From the many plains peoples to the east, they learned to hunt buffalo and to make **tepees** and feathered war bonnets.

From the Spaldings, Chief Tu-eka-kas sought ideas and knowledge. He listened to their Bible stories and liked what he heard. He, too, believed in a creator. He agreed that killing, stealing, and lying were sins. Love thy neighbor? His people were peaceful and friendly to the Cayuse, Palouse, Yakima, Umatilla, and many other neighbors.

The Nez Perce also treated strangers with kindness, including the first white

Although the Nez Perce were known for their fine horses, by 1910, the year of this photo, the Nez Perce knowledge of horse breeding was fading.

The Two Peoples Meet

On September 20, 1805, two peoples from opposite sides of a continent met for the first time at a campground called Weippe in present-day Idaho. A hunting party of six men, led by William Clark of the Corps of Discovery expedition, came across three Nee-mee-pu boys playing in a field. The boys ran back to their campsite to tell their families of the strange men who "all had eyes like dead fish." The boys had never seen light-colored eyes! And curly red hair! The leader's scraggly hair and bushy beard were the color of sunset, the boys reported.

Starving, dirty, and extra hairy, these hunters looked and smelled like animals. The Nee-mee-pu thought they had descended from dogs.

Despite first impressions, this meeting was the beginning of a warm friendship. The Nee-mee-pu fed the hungry men dried salmon and a bread made from the bulbs of wild camas lilies. They sheltered them in tepees and took excellent care of their weary horses.

For his part, Clark showered his generous hosts with gifts. He freely passed out beads, ribbons, mirrors, and other fancy items. He used his "magic" medicines to treat their ailments. His special tree bark lowered fevers. His opium from poppy flowers eased aches and pains. Clark also showed off his long-barreled rifle to warriors who hunted with bows and arrows.

William Clark wrote that his arrival at the Nez Perce camp in 1805 caused "great confusion" and "signs of fear." This painting depicts Clark (right) and Meriwether Lewis along the Missouri River.

men they ever saw. In 1805, the Nez Perce gave food, shelter, and canoes to hungry explorers from the famous Lewis and Clark expedition, formally called the Corps of Discovery. Tu-eka-kas was a young man then, perhaps twenty years old, and remembered this meeting well.

On November 11, 1839, Chief Tu-eka-kas became one of the first three Nez Perce to be **baptized**. He took on the Christian name Joseph. His wife became known as Asenath, and they remarried in a Christian ceremony. To the Spaldings, baptism and marriage before God were serious and permanent steps. In their eyes, Tu-eka-kas and the other two converts had agreed to abide by Christian rules, and no other.

The chief saw things differently. To him, Christianity was an addition to, not a replacement for, his own beliefs. In his culture, men had more than one wife—a practice strictly forbidden by the Christian church. Tu-eka-kas shared his tepee with several wives, along with Asenath, and their children, who were given Christian names.

They were called Mary, Abigail, Hannah, Manassas, Ephraim, and, of course, Joseph. Joseph's younger brother, born in 1842, was also named Joseph, but he is now remembered only by his Nee-mee-pu name: Ollokut (Frog).

Girls and Boys

As Joseph grew out of his baby years, he learned that the roles for girls and boys were sharply divided.

Who cut up the meat from freshly killed game and grilled it over an open fire? Who dug up camas roots—the bulbs of lilies— and roasted them or mashed them into bread dough? Who sewed clothing and tepee covers out of animal skins? Joseph's sisters and the other girls did all those chores and more. They learned their

American Indian or Native American?

Which name is correct—Indian, American Indian, or Native American? The people they describe use all three, but there are individuals who object one, two, or all three. A big reason is that the labels come from Europe, not from the American continents. Indian originated in 1492, with Christopher Columbus. As the story goes, the famous explorer mistakenly thought he had landed in the Indies (meaning Asia). Later, Europeans named the Western Hemisphere continents "the Americas," and so they called pre-Columbian peoples American Indians.

In the 1960s, the U.S. government invented the term *Native American*, which included people of Hawaiian and Inuit (Eskimo) descent. That's the term we use in this book, except for historic quotations and other references to nineteenth-century culture.

What term do Native Americans prefer? Their own, of course. When possible, it's best to use a nation's specific name—Nez Perce or, better yet, Nee-mee-pu.

skills working shoulder to shoulder with their mothers, aunts, and grandmothers for most of each day. The girls also helped set up and take down the camp each time the Wallowa band migrated. They sometimes had to hand-carve new tepee poles out of logs, chop by chop.

And the boys? At an early age, Joseph, Frog, and their playmates fished for salmon and hunted for elk, bear, and other game. They also tended the teeming horse and cattle herds, moving a couple thousand animals to and from their grazing grounds and along mountain trails.

On winter visits to the Spalding mission at Lapwai, all the Nez Perce and *so-ya-pu* children played and went to school together.

Joseph and Frog never learned to speak English. Yet, even without a common language, the children got along.

It was this brief but happy time at Lapwai that led Joseph to believe that the Nez Perce and white people could live in peace. He would work toward this ideal until the day he died.

The Chief's Sons

Joseph and Frog were close in age, just two years apart, but they had opposite personalities. Joseph was serious, intelligent, and well spoken. His younger brother Frog was lively and outgoing with a passion for horse racing and target shooting.

Hunting was a survival skill, and boys in many Native American cultures learned at a young age. This Lakota child (c. 1900) posed to demonstrate his name: Pulls the Bow.

What the two boys shared was the heavy load of being the chief's sons. Whereas the other boys would some day care for a family, Joseph and Frog would lead and protect the entire Wallowa band. As the older, more reserved brother, Joseph was chosen to inherit his father's title. He would become the civil chief, the leader in times and matters of peace. Frog, with his physical skills, would become the war chief. He would take charge of the warriors and serve as military adviser to his brother.

Frog earned the trust and loyalty of his future warriors by bonding with them as brothers. The boys swam, naked, in near-freezing water to toughen their bodies. They learned the tricky and dangerous skill of riding a horse hidden style. That meant they would hang their body off one side of a horse at full gallop, while shooting an arrow at a target from under the

This tricky riding style shielded the warrior's body. He shot by firing from under the horse's neck. This 1890 illustration features Plains Indians, who shared, traded, and hunted buffalo with the Nez Perce.

animal's neck. After hunting, everyone bonded further by celebrating. A chief or warrior would eat each boy's first kill as a way of honoring the boy. The ritual was a way to tell the young hunter that he would be a good provider as an adult.

As a future leader, Frog had to be stronger, braver, and more skilled than the others. His heavy load was to work extra hard to excel and to be fearless in the face of danger. Actions counted more than words.

Joseph learned to lead in a very different way. Like his father before him, he was kept at a distance from his future followers. Instead of being their friend or brother, he took responsibility for them as a parent would a child. If a child lied, stole, or did not finish chores, Joseph shouldered the blame for the child's actions. His heavy load was to act properly at all times and to convince others to do the same. How? Barking orders—"Do this!"—did not work. The Nez Perce believed no one could tell another person how to live his or her life.

Joseph needed to find softer words that kept people working toward the common good. But what if children did not listen to his words? How could he keep them from making mistakes and causing trouble? The ability to convince others would turn out to be the most important skill for young Joseph to master.

At the age of seven, he saw the bloody result when warriors did not listen to their chiefs.

A Mass Murder

On November 29, 1847, enraged Cayuse warriors killed Marcus and Narcissa Whitman and eleven other white settlers. Like the Spaldings, the Whitmans were missionaries. Their mission was in the heart of Cayuse country, near Walla Walla in what is now Washington State.

What triggered this massacre?

The problems began when the Whitmans lured a flood of settlers from the East into the Walla Walla area. The couple led wagon trains packed with families along the famous Oregon Trail, a route that spanned half the country from the central plains to the west coast. One trip, called the Great Migration of 1843, brought in a thousand people, all at once.

Over the next four years, the sudden rush of settlers created a plague of problems. The settlers carried the germ for measles. Their bodies had natural defenses to fight this common European disease. But the Cayuse did not, and measles wiped out entire families. Some warriors thought the settlers were spreading measles on purpose, especially when missionaries could offer no cure.

This wood engraving dramatizes the 1847 ax murder of Marcus Whitman. Cayuse warriors shot his wife to death and then killed eleven other settlers.

Another source of tension was that the Whitmans and Spaldings treated some native men as laborers. They forced the Cayuse to work the fields and build houses. The men balked at doing what they considered women's work. The missionaries whipped those who refused to obey their orders.

Those and other conflicts sent the blood of warriors to the boiling point. The men killed the white settlers to avenge the abuse and insults.

Hearing of the massacre, the Spaldings closed their mission in Lapwai and fled for their lives. As they left, a group of Nez Perce warriors protected the couple, hoping to avoid more bloodshed. The Lapwai mission was soon looted and destroyed.

Chief Tu-eka-kas moved his people back to their homelands in the Wallowa and Imnaha River valleys for good. The murders taught Joseph an important lesson. He realized that, in order to

Pioneers on the Oregon Trail walked 2,000 miles across plains and mountains. Many starving families stopped at the Whitman mission for supplies. Narcissa Whitman (1808–1847) complained of having no food left, except for potatoes.

live peacefully, white people and native people had to treat one another as equals.

Thunder Rising

Late one autumn, after arriving at Imnaha, Tu-eka-kas asked young Joseph to go discover his *wayakin*, or powerful spirit guide. The Nez Perce believed that everyone had a unique and personal guide who protected him or her for life. The *wayakin* usually took the form of an imagined animal or a natural object, which then became the person's name.

Like other young boys between the ages of nine and fifteen, Joseph went on a **vision quest**. He walked into the mountains by himself, empty-handed, and didn't eat for days. He slept on the ground under the shelter of trees. Hungry, afraid, and half asleep, he waited for his *wayakin* to reveal itself in a dream.

Joseph's vision quest was a success. He returned to the winter long house, a permanent winter shelter that all the families shared. There, in a ceremony, he announced his new *wayakin* name: Hin-mah-too-yah-lat-kekt. The Nez Perce word is hard to translate into English. It means something close to "Thunder Rising Over Distant Mountains" or "Thunder Traveling to Loftier Heights" or "Thunder Crossing the Water and Fading on Distant Slopes."

He realized that, in order to live peacefully, white people and native people had to treat one another as equals.

The image fit. Even as a child, Joseph had a quiet but powerful presence—like distant thunder. He could keep a cool head while others raged. In his calm, strong way, the future chief of the Wallowa band earned respect. He gave respect, too, by listening to others and showing a true concern for their well-being. Mutual respect and well-chosen words, he found, were his keys to leadership.

Frog's tools were earning the trust and loyalty of his future warriors. His men would have to go into battle together, risking their lives for one another.

Together, the chief's sons would need all their skills to face the difficult challenges ahead of them.

CHAPTER 2

Speaking With Two Tongues

[Our fathers] told us to treat all men as they treated us, that we should never be the first to break a bargain, that we should only speak the truth.

The Christian missionaries had taught young Joseph that telling a lie was a sin. The Nez Perce felt the same way. They called this serious offense "speaking with two tongues." Being truthful was especially important during councils— the formal meetings of leaders. The Nez Perce had an interesting way of trusting one another. If a person said something once, it could be the truth or a lie. If the person said it a second time, it could still be the truth or a lie. Yet if the words were spoken a third time, they were considered the truth.

How did the *so-ya-pu* deal with truth and lies? At age fourteen, Joseph was about to learn their way of speaking at councils.

The Council of 1855

On May 29, 1855, Isaac Stevens, governor of the new Washington Territory, called all the native peoples in the region to a council. Stevens was an army engineer from the East. Though surprisingly short, he had a tough, no-nonsense attitude and a drive to win whatever goal he

Though limited in height, Governor Isaac Stevens (1818–1862) had a powerful presence and made bold promises to the Native Americans of the Northwest.

tackled. For one example, he graduated at the top of his class at the U.S. Military Academy at West Point.

Tu-eka-kas, now in his sixties, felt sure that the council had little to do with his remote band. So far, his people had had few conflicts with white settlers. Still, he was mildly curious about what Stevens had in mind, so he agreed to attend the council, along with half a dozen other Nez Perce chiefs. Tu-eka-kas led young Joseph and others of the Wallowa band to the meeting place near Walla Walla, Washington. This was Cayuse country, not far from the location of the Whitman massacre.

Cayuse, Yakima, Walla Wallas, and other groups arrived over a couple of days and camped at a distance from the governor's central tent in a forest clearing. With settlers rapidly filling their lands, they had had many bloody encounters with white people and felt wary and distrustful of them.

The Nez Perce bands chose to enter the clearing in grand style together. Joseph watched as the warriors staged a noisy, colorful parade to show off their strength and numbers. The men were dressed as if for battle—stripped to their loincloths, with brightly painted bodies. They wore feathers and decorated their horses with beautiful beadwork. Hundreds of braves rode, single file, around the white men standing under a central tent. The riders circled three times, as per custom, beating their shields and shouting heart-stopping war whoops.

Joseph noted that the governor had brought with him about a hundred men, many of them soldiers. In stark contrast to the nearly naked warriors, these *so-ya-pu* were stiffly dressed from head to toe in suits, uniforms, and hats.

As the council began, Governor Stevens found his little group surrounded by some five thousand Native Americans, about half of which were Nez Perce. If he was shaken by the noisy Nez Perce parade and the sheer numbers of Native Americans, he didn't show it. He knew that he had the entire U.S. government behind him. And he had a key ally right beside him—a Nez Perce leader named Lawyer.

The "Head Chief"

Lawyer had been one of the three Nee-mce-pu boys who, in 1805, made first contact with William Clark's hunting party. He earned his English name because he spoke the language well and had a talent for swaying others to his side. Now middle-aged, Lawyer was a Christian Nez Perce who had plunged—heart, soul, and wallet—into the *so-ya-pu* lifestyle. He wore western clothes topped by a tall, fancy hat with three large feathers on top. Though he kept his black hair long, he prayed every day and farmed a plot of land, just like his settler neighbors in Lapwai, Idaho.

Lawyer added fancy touches to his western clothes. Sometimes he topped his towering hat with ostrich feathers and carried a big, colorful handbag. His "Sunday best" was a shiny suit with a fluffy bowtie.

At the council, Stevens appointed Lawyer as the so-called head chief who would speak for all the Nez Perce. He wanted to avoid dealing with each chief separately, and he knew the Christian convert would take his side. Lawyer had proven his loyalty by helping U.S. soldiers catch five Cayuse warriors blamed for the Whitman massacre. Most of the men were innocent, but the U.S. Army hanged them anyway.

The traditional chiefs, including Tu-eka-kas, scoffed at the idea of a so-called head chief. There was no such thing in all of Nez Perce history. Each chief spoke only for himself and for his band of people. Tu-eka-kas led the Wallowas, but he had little to do with the dozen or so other Nez Perce bands. To the traditional leaders, Lawyer was not even much of a chief. He was more *so-ya-pu* than Nez Perce and a subchief at best.

Lawyer understood the independent role of chiefs but did nothing to correct Stevens. By working with the mighty U.S. government, he stood to gain both power and wealth.

Stevens's Offer

To butter up the crowd, Stevens started the council by making generous offers and promises. First, he pointed to a shed full of food, blankets, pots, and other gifts. Families could take anything they needed, he said, and eat as much as they liked. Then he described the great life everyone could have with free homes, schools and teachers, doctors, saw mills, and fine goods. They would all receive a large sum of cash from the U.S. President Franklin Pierce. U.S. soldiers would protect them from their Native American enemies, including the feared Blackfeet and Bannock—aggressive groups that had fought the Nez Perce. They would also help bring criminals to justice, including settlers who broke the law.

About Chiefs and Councils

The Nez Perce were never united under a single chief. Each independent band had several leaders who made decisions together at councils. There was generally a civil chief like Joseph, a war chief like Frog, several young subchiefs, and warriors who had proven themselves in battle. Women did not attend the meetings but gave their opinions to the men who did.

The point of a council was for the leaders to speak their hearts, not to give orders. No one told anyone what to do. All voices were heard, especially elderly ones, whose experience was highly valued. The idea was to state an opinion and see what others thought. Those who agreed silently pulled their blanket over their shoulders as a signal of approval. Those who disagreed or thought they had a better idea spoke up freely.

The group usually came to a common decision, based on whose words had carried the most weight. Still, individuals were free to go their own way. Depending on the outcome of a decision, the balance of power could shift, especially if lives were lost. The person who put forth the failed idea had a weaker voice at the next council.

Chief Joseph's greatest skill wasn't as a warrior or a military genius, as some people of the day mistakenly believed. He would shine as an orator, a speaker who could sway others with well-chosen words.

This c. 1890 print depicts a chief holding a council to announce the arrival of tall ships, which are out of our view. The ships' commander is explorer Christopher Columbus.

One out of four Cherokees died on the Trail of Tears, a long, forced march to Indian Territory (now Oklahoma). This 1942 oil painting portrays their misery. Rumors of many such broken promises and lost homelands reached the Northwest.

Stevens claimed that many other groups in the East were now happy and rich, thanks to the U.S. government. Incredibly, he mentioned the Cherokee. In 1838, seventeen years earlier, the Cherokee had been forced to leave their Smoky Mountain homeland. As they walked the long, grueling Trail of Tears to Indian Territory (Oklahoma), many died from disease and exhaustion. The survivors were miserable and poor.

Stevens was speaking with two tongues—and then some. However, few Native Americans at the council knew directly about the Cherokee's plight.

Tu-eka-kas and the other chiefs began to wonder: What was the cost to them of this "happy" life? What would the governor demand in return?

Finally, after days of promising the sun and the moon, Stevens pointed to a small area of land on a map. This land, he declared, would belong to the government and be open to settlement. All other Native American lands in the region would be off-limits to white settlers. All the chiefs had to do, he said, was sign a **treaty** stating the terms of the agreement.

Lawyer quickly offered to sign, as Stevens knew he would. Then, out of the blue, an old and respected war chief named Ip-pak-ness Way-hay-ken (Looking Glass) arrived at the council. He rode in on a swift horse with three of his best warriors. Without waiting to dismount, Looking Glass urged the other chiefs to hold their own council before making any agreements with white people. They all agreed.

Tu-eka-kas and Joseph noted that the plot of land the government wanted was nowhere near their Wallowa River valley.

Looking Glass was a boy at the 1855 treaty council when his father of the same name made a bold stand. He is pictured here in the eventful year 1877.

It was their understanding that, under this treaty, they could keep their homeland free from settlers forever. To them, there didn't seem to be a downside. Even Looking Glass, whose Nez Perce homeland was similarly off-limits, found this sweet deal hard to turn down.

Unfortunately for the Palouse and Walla Wallas, the government's proposed plot included all of their homeland. The plot extended into parts of other groups' lands, too.

On June 11, 1855, Tu-eka-kas, Looking Glass, and most of the other chiefs each signed Stevens's treaty by marking the paper with an *X*. The chiefs who lost their land likely felt they had no choice. They had experienced the army's crushing power firsthand. In addition, they probably didn't fully understand the terms. The treaty was written in English, a language they could not read or understand.

Lawyer, who could read English, happily signed the document with a full signature. In Stevens's eyes, that name alone sealed the deal. Still, the U.S. government wanted to gather as many signers as they could to strengthen their land claim.

Almost as soon as the ink was dry, the agreement was broken. Newspaper articles invited settlers to stake claims in the newly opened land—with no mention of treaty borders. Years passed, and the promised goods and money never arrived. Even Lawyer came to admit that the treaty was a sham.

Young Joseph learned that *so-ya-pu* boldly and easily spoke with two tongues, even at councils.

The groups who lost their land went to war against the U.S. government. Tu-eka-kas watched the conflicts from an uneasy distance. He didn't want to risk lives in a fight he did not consider his own. The U.S. Army quashed the uprising within three years.

Gold Changes Everything

On February 20, 1860, a miner named Elias Pierce discovered gold dust in the Clearwater River. This jackpot was not far from Lapwai and the former Spalding mission in Idaho. It was also right in the middle of Nez Perce land. The Treaty of 1855 clearly showed that the land belonged to the Lapwai bands.

No matter. Gold changed everything. Within a day, the first tent city sprang up. The miners raised canvas shelters, not wood houses, in part to skirt the law. Speaking with two tongues, they could claim they were campers, not settlers. They were just passing through Nez Perce land, they pretended, while robbing it of its riches. The miners would eventually collect some $3 million worth of gold. That windfall would be worth about $77 million today.

Just as gold attracted miners, rich miners drew thousands of traders, gamblers, outlaws, con men, and other fortune seekers.

The California Gold Rush (1848–1855) ended the same year Tu-eka-kas signed a treaty with the U.S. In the early 1860s, thousands of miners flocked to the Northwest.

Saloonkeepers brought in wagons full of whiskey. These illegal settlers soon dropped all pretense and boldly built **boomtowns** with names such as Pierce, Elk City, and Lewiston. Lewiston alone grew to twelve hundred people in just one month.

Lawyer and other Christian Nez Perce struck it rich along with the gold diggers. They traded and sold goods. They guided the miners in the wilderness and ferried them across rivers for money.

This jackpot was . . . right in the middle of Nez Perce land.

Meanwhile, newspapers reported increasing conflicts between whites and "wild Indians," meaning non-Christians. These run-ins were often whiskey-fueled and lopsided. The whiskey caused people to act, often violently, without thinking or caring. The conflicts were lopsided because crimes against native peoples went unpunished. Yet if a Native American harmed or killed a white person, he or she was jailed or hanged.

Violence gripped the lawless region in knots.

Joseph watched the conflicts with interest, but, as his father had, from a distance. Just out of his teen years, he stood six feet tall. His brother Frog, now a full-fledged warrior, stood even taller, a well-muscled six feet, two inches.

The two young men understood that the traditional chiefs in Idaho could do little to stop the invasion. Joseph likened it to reversing the flow of a raging river—an impossible feat. So far, their group's Wallowa River valley in Oregon was too high, too snowy in winter, and too remote to attract anyone but Nez Perce. The entrance trail was too steep and narrow for wagons. The rivers were flecked with pink salmon, not yellow gold.

Not a single settler had planted roots there—yet.

CHAPTER 3

A People Divided

I learned then that we were . . . like deer. They were like grizzly bears. We had a small country. Their country was large.

Joseph understood that the lands of the U.S. government were far larger than any native homeland. Yet he had never traveled beyond the Northwest. He could not possibly imagine how vast and fast-growing the country really was.

In 1861, the United States of America spanned coast to coast with some thirty-five million people. However, the country was split sharply in two. In the East, a bloody Civil War between the North and the South was raging.

The war didn't spill way out into the West, but neither did much of the payment from the 1855 treaty. Joseph's band saw none of Stevens's brightly promised money and goods. Congress had taken six years to **ratify** and fulfill the treaty. By then, the government was waging a costly war and couldn't afford to send much cash to the West. The trickle of goods

The soldiers in blue are Union troops. This print shows the Battle of Gettysburg from their point of view. The Civil War left too few troops in the West to keep law and order.

that did arrive was shabby. Most of the meager payment was given to or taken by the Christian Nez Perce in Lapwai. The groups that lost their homelands in 1855—the Walla Wallas, Palouse, and others—were left out in the cold.

Then, incredibly, the U.S. government demanded even more land—a *lot* more land.

The Thief Treaty

In 1862, Congress passed the Homestead Act, which offered free land, in 160-acre plots, to settlers who agreed to build on it. From opening day, a frenzied land rush, like a gold rush, swept across the plains. In less than a year, this land fever reached the Northwest. Paving the way was the new Superintendent of Indian Affairs, a white man named Calvin Hale.

In 1862, homesteaders like this Nebraska family snapped up free 160-acre plots of wilderness. To keep the land, they had to build a home and a working farm within five years.

In June 1863, Hale called the regional groups to a council at Fort Lapwai. He opened the meeting with an outrageous demand. He said the government would take ninety percent of all Nez Perce land for homesteaders. Every Nez Perce family, in all the Northwest, would have to live on a small **reservation** in the Idaho panhandle. In return, each family would receive a house and a plot of land to farm. The plots were far too tiny to raise herds of horses and cattle, the main livelihood of the Nez Perce.

The price for giving up some *five thousand square miles* of land? Hale offered to pay all the Nez Perce bands $262,000, or about $4 million in today's money. The cost of moving all the families would be deducted from this fee, he added.

Tu-eka-kas and other traditional chiefs were furious when they heard the terms. They refused to have anything to do with Hale's shameful land grab. They called it a "thief treaty." Joseph would later liken the raw deal to having a neighbor who sells your horses: The neighbor keeps the money. The buyer takes the horses. You end up with nothing.

Every Nez Perce family, in all the Northwest, would have to live on a small reservation in the Idaho panhandle.

Like Governor Stevens in 1855, Hale appointed Lawyer as the so-called head chief. With none of the traditional Nez Perce chiefs present, Lawyer signed the treaty. So did fifty-one other Christian Nez Perce who already had farms at Lapwai. They were happy to "sell" land that belonged to non-Christian Nez Perce. Hale claimed the signatures—many of them simple Xs—were legal "proof" that all the Nez Perce people agreed to the terms.

"Friendly" Versus "Hostile"

The thief treaty split the Nez Perce people in half forever. The signers and their followers, all Christians, numbered in the hundreds. They became known as the treaty Nez Perce. Settlers and soldiers called them "friendly Indians."

The non-treaty Nez Perce, including Joseph's Wallowa band, continued to live in their traditional way on their ancestors' land. Also numbering in the hundreds, whites referred to them as "hostile Indians," even in government reports and newspaper articles.

To defy the government's land grab, Tu-eka-kas staked out the borders of the Wallowa River valley homeland. He built seven large, rock posts along the ridges surrounding the narrow entry trail, making sure any unwelcome settlers could clearly see the markers.

Tu-eka-kas also angrily tore up his Bible—a gift from the missionary Henry Spalding. He wanted nothing to do with Christians who spoke with two tongues. He and his sons took up the Dreamer religion, an extreme version of their traditional beliefs. The Dreamers believed in a future in which native peoples would rise up and reclaim their greatness. This hopeful outlook was quickly gaining steam in reaction to the ever-growing tidal wave of white settlers. The more powerless the Nez Perce felt, the more strongly they clung to a rosy future.

Chief Joseph would wear his high-swept Dreamer hair for the rest of his life. For this portrait (c. 1880), he combined his chief's sash and beaded necklace with a western shirt.

The Creator and the Dreamers

Christian missionaries, including the Spaldings and Whitmans, spread their religion around the world. It was easy to carry a Bible, say prayers, and build a church anywhere. The Nez Perce religion, by contrast, was not at all portable. It was deeply and permanently rooted in the land of one's birth.

At the core of the religion was a Creator, who made the world to perfection. The earth that gave people life and kept them alive with its bounty of food was the mother. When people died, the mother reclaimed them. Cutting into the land to plant crops was like cutting into your mother's flesh. Diverting a river for crops was like changing the course of your mother's blood. Above all, you didn't leave your mother. And you certainly didn't sell her for goods and money. The land where you were born, where your ancestors were buried, was a permanent and eternal part of you.

The hardcore believers were called the Dreamers. One of their **prophets**, Smohalla, explained to a white soldier named E. L. Huggins, "My young men shall never work. Men who work cannot dream, and wisdom comes to us in dreams."

The Dreamers preached that a new god would come. This god would bring back all the dead native peoples, who would prevail over all enemies. This message of hope and triumph caught fire among a people whose land and culture were being overrun.

Joseph had always worn his long, black hair in two braids. He swept his bangs into a lock that rose high above his forehead, held in place by grease. Frog followed suit. This towering forelock was a symbol of their Dreamer beliefs.

Death of a Chief

For eight years after the thief treaty, the Wallowa band lived in relative peace thanks to the remoteness of their land. In August 1871, as Tu-eka-kas lay dying, his people still had the Wallowa River valley to themselves. The old chief, though nearly blind, saw that it couldn't last.

As Joseph would recount later, his father pleaded with him to never accept gifts from white people. If he did, white people would say that he had sold something.

"Always remember that your father never sold his country," he said. "You must stop your ears [not listen] whenever you are asked to sign a treaty selling your home."

"A few years more," the ailing chief continued, "and white men will be all around you. They have their eyes on this land. My son, never forget my dying words. This country holds your father's body. Never sell the bones of your father and your mother."

Joseph, Frog, and the Wallowa band buried their chief in the soil of the Creator. As a grave marker, they hung the framed skin of a horse that they believed would carry the chief to the spirit world.

Now came the time for Joseph and Frog to lead their people into a tense, uncertain future.

CHAPTER 4

Young Chief Joseph

Our fathers were born here. Here they lived, here they died, here are their graves. We will never leave them.

In the year 1871, Joseph had a wife and six-year-old daughter. At age thirty-one, he was the youngest of the non-treaty chiefs. Yet, with Frog by his side, he headed the largest Nez Perce band, more than three hundred in number. They owned a couple thousand excellent horses and cattle and the best fishery in the region. They had no need for farms or government handouts.

Knowing his turn would come, Joseph watched how other chiefs dealt with *so-ya-pu* intruders. The band most overrun with miners and outlaws and settlers lived along the Salmon River, south of Lapwai. The leader was Chief Peo-peo Hih-hih (White Bird). In his mid-sixties, he was the oldest of the non-treaty chiefs. Still battle-fit, the war chief wore a fancy hat with an eagle wing that hung down in front of his face. He hated and distrusted the *so-ya-pu*. He vowed to never hand over his land. He would fight if he had to but hoped to avoid war against a powerful enemy.

White Bird's neighbor, in the hills between the Snake and Salmon rivers, was Chief Too-hool-hool-zote (Grating Sound). Grating Sound spoke with a low, gruff voice. He had broad shoulders, a thick neck, and a deep chest rippled with muscles. A passionate Dreamer, he was defiant and hostile toward whites. The blood of his warriors ran hot. Yet he, too, stopped short of triggering a war.

Chief Looking Glass was the son of the chief by the same name who rode into the 1855 council at Walla Walla. He took over the band after his father died. His group lived along the Clearwater River in Idaho, not far from Lapwai. Looking Glass was a tall, seasoned bison hunter about forty years old. He had a forceful personality with plenty of opinions to share. When it came to the *so-ya-pu*, though, he chose to ignore them. To avoid trouble, he moved his people just inside the borders of the thief treaty.

He vowed to never hand over his land.

Joseph's Turn

Since the Whitman massacre, there had been much more bloodshed. Violence led to more violence, Joseph believed. Yet he had promised his father he would guard the land, no matter what. He would have to stand his ground forcefully but keep the peace, too. This was a dangerous tightrope for a young chief to walk.

"A few more years," his father had warned. But the first settlers in the Wallowa River valley arrived within months, not years. In the spring of 1872, Joseph's band returned from the long house in the Imnaha River valley to find cabins and corrals along its beautiful blue lake and fishing creeks. A handful of ranchers had moved onto the snow-covered land over the winter.

Joseph asked them to please leave.

The ranchers refused. They mentioned the Treaty of 1863.

Joseph countered that his people had not signed that thief treaty. They had only signed the Treaty of 1855, which made the Wallowa River valley off-limits to settlers, forever.

The ranchers still refused to leave.

Joseph explained that the Creator had given this land to his people. They were born here. Their fathers and mothers were buried here. They could never and would never leave their ancestors.

The ranchers knew nothing of a Creator—and didn't care.

This tense tug-of-war stretched into summer. More ranchers moved in to take advantage of the valley's lush grazing grass, bringing the total to about forty.

On August 14, 1872, Joseph and Frog called them all to a council. After three days of fruitless talk, the ranchers summoned John Monteith, the government agent in charge of the Nez Perce region. Monteith would serve as the Nez Perce agent from 1871 to 1879. Part of his job was to solve conflicts peacefully.

Agent Monteith (standing) relied on Christian Nez Perce to talk their non-treaty cousins into accepting white ways. Archie Lawyer (son of Chief Lawyer) (left), Mark Williams (center), and James Reuben (right), are suited up for this 1890 photo.

Government Agents

The U.S. government assigned agents to a region to solve problems between whites and native peoples and to dole out money and goods to treaty signers. Because these agents worked for the government, and not for Native Americans, the welfare of their charges was not a top priority. Many corrupt agents were in it only for themselves. They stole the money and sold the goods they were supposed to pass out to Native Americans.

President Ulysses S. Grant was disgusted by this corruption and waste of taxpayer dollars. So, in 1868, he tried to end it by turning over the role of the agents to devoutly religious people, like the Presbyterian John Monteith. He called it his Peace Policy.

Grant hoped the religious agents would pick up where missionaries had left off and convert the Native Americans into law-abiding, Christian farmers. But not all the agents knew what they were doing. And not all of them were honest and caring. Some were just as corrupt as the earlier government agents.

Most agents also showed little or no respect for native cultures, especially their religions. They believed the white way of living was the only proper way. Why would someone live in a tepee instead of a house? Given suits and coats and dresses, why would anyone wear buckskin, moccasins, and blankets? Agents failed to see that many traditional groups, like the Wallowa band, were happy, healthy, and even wealthy in their way of life.

Many agents treated Native Americans unfairly. In this 1890 cartoon, a fat agent is loaded with money bags. A thin, raggedy Native American holds a package labeled "starvation rations."

Land Granted

Monteith was tall and thin with a bushy black beard and pasty white skin. He thought all Native Americans were better off living like the "friendly" ones. He even brought along James Reuben, a treaty Nez Perce and Joseph's brother-in-law, to help make that point.

Monteith and Reuben tried to pressure Joseph into moving to Lapwai, where there would be no trouble. Joseph repeated, calmly but firmly, his legal and spiritual claim to the land. Once again, he stated that his father had not signed the 1863 thief treaty.

Neither side budged. Even so, after the meeting, Monteith wrote a letter to his bosses in Washington, D.C.—the officials in charge of Native American affairs. He advised, "If there is any way by which the Wallowa River valley could be kept for the Indians, I would recommend that it be done."

Monteith's reason for making this request was neither legal nor spiritual. It was **economic**. He knew the high mountain land was worthless for farming. Ranching and fishing were the only ways to make a living there. Let the Nez Perce have their grazing grass and salmon, he reasoned, and go after good farmland elsewhere instead.

His letter did help produce a fix. In 1873, President Ulysses Grant signed an order to split the Wallowa River valley in half—one

President Ulysses Grant (1822–1885) said that the best way to get rid of a bad law was to strictly enforce it. His idea was that people treated unfairly would fight to undo the law.

half for the settlers and one half for the Nez Perce. After all, there was plenty of grazing grass and salmon to go around. Unfortunately the fix turned out to be more like a bandage—a temporary patch—than a permanent cure. The disease of hatred and mistrust continued to fester, with each side insisting that the other side should leave the valley.

The tense standoff extended through 1873, 1874, and into 1875. Each spring, when the Nez Perce returned to Wallowa, they found more cabins and corrals. What's more, ranchers stole Nez Perce horses and cattle and got away with it. They boldly built a road right past the stone border markers that Tu-eka-kas had built. They even charged a toll! When tempers boiled over, Monteith called in U.S. troops to cool them down.

Under pressure from the ranchers, on June 10, 1875, President Grant took back his order to split the valley. The settlers believed all of Wallowa was now theirs. In Joseph's view, the Treaty of 1855 still made his people's land off-limits.

Talk or Fight?

Uncertain what to do next, the young chief asked for a council with four older chiefs: Looking Glass, White Bird, Grating Sound, and Tipi-yah-lan-ah Kah-aw-pu (Eagle from the Light). Eagle from the Light's band lived in the Bitterroot Mountains on the Idaho-Montana border. His people, too, had put up with many injustices at the hands of white settlers. Finally fed up, Eagle

After the 1863 thief treaty, Chief Eagle from the Light angrily moved his people from Idaho to Montana. By the time of this photo, c. 1877, he had decided not to fight the United States.

from the Light joined Grating Sound and White Bird in arguing for war.

Joseph and Looking Glass, the chief who chose to ignore the settlers, disagreed. Even if all the Nez Perce bands united, they would lose against the U.S. Army. The Cayuse had paid a steep price for their defeat—many people were killed and all their land was stolen. Joseph decided that talking was still his best option.

He pleaded his case to the new army officer in charge of the entire Northwest, General Oliver Howard. Howard was a veteran of the American Civil War who had lost his right arm in battle. He was more familiar with the treaty Nez Perce Christians at Lapwai than Joseph's remote band. He expected the Wallowa men to be savages. Instead, he was impressed by the young chief's calm intelligence and "superior nature."

As a soldier, General Howard noted with approval that Chief Joseph and his men were neatly dressed and tall and sturdy.

Howard later wrote, "Joseph put his large black eyes on my face and maintained a fixed look for some time. It did not appear to me as an audacious [bold] stare, but I thought he was trying to open the windows of his heart to me."

Joseph laid out his concerns about the ranchers in thoughtful, well-reasoned arguments. Howard listened, but he made no promises. As a general, he had to follow the orders of the commander in chief, the president of the United States. And President Grant had clearly ordered the Nez Perce to leave the Wallowa River valley.

After the meeting, despite their opposing views, General Howard considered Joseph to be a man of honor.

A Cold-Blooded Murder

Yet another tense spring passed. Then, on June 23, 1876, ranchers A. B. Findley and Wells McNall shot and killed Joseph's close friend, Wil-haut-yah (Wind Blowing). Findley thought Wind Blowing had stolen his horses—but the animals were found a few days later. Findley and McNall's act turned out to be the cold-blooded murder of an innocent man.

Monteith, the government agent, agreed. He pleaded with Joseph and Frog to keep their warriors from seeking revenge. He promised them that the government would handle the matter fairly.

Weeks passed, and nothing happened. Findley and McNall remained free. In August 1876, Joseph twice had dinner at the Findley cabin, even playing with the rancher's children. He hoped to convince the murderer to turn himself in or leave the valley. Findley refused.

Joseph continued to meet with Monteith and the ranchers, hoping to bring the killers to justice and reclaim his homeland.

Despite these talks, more cabins were built, more livestock was stolen, and the two killers still went unpunished. Several times, Frog gathered his warriors for target-shooting practice and war dances. The loud gatherings lasted all night long.

The settlers became alarmed at what they saw as a threat. Fueling their fears was a shocking massacre that had occurred in Montana that same summer. In June, Lakota warriors had trapped and killed every soldier in General George Custer's unit at the Battle of the Little Bighorn. Their leader was the famous Chief Ta-tan-ka-Iyo-tanka (Sitting Bull). Like the Nez Perce, the Lakota were fighting to keep their land.

The slaughter of troops reported at Custer's Last Stand caused some soldiers and settlers to call for bloody revenge on all Indians. A hotheaded rancher named Gerard Cochran foolishly bragged to a couple of Nez Perce women that he would **scalp** all their people, including Joseph. Other ranchers openly made similar threats.

Monteith wrote to General Howard, asking for troops to keep the peace. Howard sent in the **cavalry** and arranged another meeting with Joseph.

"Since my [friend's] life had been taken in Wallowa Valley," Joseph said firmly, "his body buried there, and the earth there had drunk up his blood, the valley is more sacred to me than ever before."

George Custer wore a wide-brimmed hat over his curly red hair and a form-fitting uniform with tall, shiny boots. A veteran of the Civil War and Indian wars, he often struck this defiant pose in photographs to play up his image as a tough fighter. Instead, he's known for making a fatal battlefield blunder called Custer's Last Stand.

Custer's Last Stand

On June 25, 1876, General George Custer (1839–1876) and his Seventh Cavalry Regiment attacked a village of non-treaty Lakota (also called Sioux) at Little Bighorn, Montana. The attack was part of the ongoing Indian wars to make the West safe for white settlers. Of course, to Native Americans, the so-called Indian wars were about keeping the government from stealing their land.

To Custer's surprise, the Lakota village housed 1,500 warriors led by Chief Sitting Bull. The Lakota cornered Custer's cavalry unit and slaughtered all 225 men, including the general. The one-sided battle would go down in both history and legend as Custer's Last Stand.

Fearing a counterattack, Sitting Bull (c. 1831–1890) fled with his people to Canada, just beyond reach of the U.S. Army. By the following summer, 1877, several thousand warriors were camped just over the border. The army's biggest fear was that Sitting Bull would unite Native Americans and return to the United States to wage an all-out war.

That never happened. In 1890, the Indian wars ended when U.S. soldiers killed Lakota men, women, and children at the Massacre at Wounded Knee in South Dakota.

Books, songs, and artwork (such as this 1889 lithograph) usually cast Custer's Last Stand as a heroic defeat. In truth, it was a hopeless, bloody disaster caused by a military mistake.

Sitting Bull was fearless from the day of his first battle at age 14 to his last one in 1890.

The *so-ya-pu* murderers must leave, Frog added bluntly.

Howard assured the brothers that he would bring Findley and McNall to justice. He further promised that a **commission** would find a solution to the legal claims over the land. His aide, Major Henry Clay Wood, had previously concluded that the law was on Joseph's side. On January 8, 1876, Wood reported that, since Tu-eka-kas never signed the Treaty of 1863, the government's claim to the land was "imperfect and incomplete." That left the Treaty of 1855, the one that protected the Wallowa River valley from settlers, still in force. Wood called President Grant's decision to make the Nez Perce leave a blunder, if not a crime.

Howard wrote in his report to Washington, D.C., "I think it a great mistake to take from Joseph and his band of Nez Perce Indians that valley. . . . Possibly Congress can . . . let these really peaceable Indians have their poor valley for their own."

A Show of Force

Once again, nothing was done to settle the open disputes. Some of Frog's warriors cried for blood to avenge the murder of Wind Blowing. To Joseph's dismay, they harassed the settlers by stealing horses and picking fights.

Joseph had to act. He and Frog came up with a plan. Accounts of what happened next differ. One thing that's clear is that on September 2, 1876, almost ten weeks after the murder, Frog rallied his warriors. Sixty braves, their bodies covered in war paint, mounted their best horses. Some witnesses say their guns were poised and loaded. Others say the warriors had their weapons slung on their backs, out of reach, showing they did not intend to attack.

Frog left behind few photos and little information about his life. In this 1877 portrait, his hair is greased into a tall Dreamer forelock, and he wears the beaded necklaces of a chief.

In any case, the ranchers believed the Nez Perce meant war. Greatly outnumbered, a well-armed group hid inside the McNall cabin. The warriors rode to a hill overlooking the ranch and lined up along the ridge.

Joseph would later explain, "When the white men were few and we were strong, we could have killed them all off. But the Nez Perce wished to live in peace."

By some accounts, the daughter of Wind Blowing, the murder victim, walked boldly down to the McNall cabin. She pushed open the door and asked to see her father's killers. Ranchers slammed the door in her face.

Joseph asked to see the rancher who bragged about scalping him. The trembling Cochran came forth. Joseph calmly but firmly stated that the Nez Perce were peaceful but they would not stand for murderers and illegal settlers on their land. He demanded that all the settlers leave the valley. They had one week, he added. Then Frog led his warriors away.

Troops arrived a week later to prevent an all-out war. The settlers still refused to leave their homesteads, but McNall and Findley were finally arrested. They would later be **acquitted** for lack of evidence. In that year of 1876 alone, more than thirty Nez Perce murders by white people went unpunished.

The recent threat of war caused Howard to have a change of heart. He now firmly believed that Joseph's band would be safer and better off at Lapwai, far from the angry Wallowa settlers. In November 1876, he announced a plan to carry out President Grant's orders. General Howard told Chief Joseph to move his people to the reservation by April 1.

Joseph was outraged. He replied, "All I have to say is that I love my country. We will not sell the land. We will not give up the land."

CHAPTER 5

Showing the Rifle

I did not want my people killed. I did not want anybody killed. . . . I would give up everything rather than have the blood of white men on the hands of my people.

The April 1 deadline to move to Lapwai came and went. Meanwhile, Joseph's band made their way back up to the Wallowa River valley from their winter camp.

In May 1877, General Howard called for a council with the non-treaty Nez Perce. Having met Joseph a number of times, he regarded the well-spoken, thirty-six-year-old chief as the main leader. He often referred to all the traditional Nez Perce as Joseph's people. Joseph introduced Howard to the elderly and respected White Bird, to Grating Sound, the devout Dreamer, and to other chiefs. But the general continued to focus on Joseph.

Built in 1862, Fort Lapwai's original purpose was to protect Nez Perce land from miners and settlers. By 1877 (left), it was the headquarters for moving Native Americans onto the reservation.

The council took place at Fort Lapwai. The rickety buildings there housed about a hundred and twenty poorly trained U.S. soldiers. Money was so tight that there weren't enough bullets for proper target practice.

As in previous councils, the hundreds of non-treaty warriors were dressed for battle, their faces painted bright red. They staged the traditional loud parade, circling three times around the grounds.

Unfazed, Howard opened the council with a bold command. He ordered the non-treaty chiefs to move their people to Lapwai. Though he had let the April 1 deadline slide, this time he would accept no other outcome. This new order came straight from Washington, he added.

Perrin Whitman translated Grating Sound's speech into English for General Howard.

As always, the sole goal of the non-treaty chiefs was to keep their land. They vowed never to sign a two-tongued treaty. To Howard's surprise, they chose Grating Sound, not Joseph, to state their case. Howard had mistakenly thought Chief Grating Sound was only a **shaman**, or medicine man—not a chief. In his gruff voice, Grating Sound spoke words of fire and passion in the Nez Perce language. Perrin Whitman, whose uncle Marcus Whitman was murdered by Cayuse, translated the growling words into English.

Grating Sound's Speech

Grating Sound accused Howard of ordering the Nez Perce around like children. He asked, mockingly, about the source of these orders, this so-called Washington. "Is he a chief or a common man, a house or a place? Leave Mr. Washington—that is, if he is a man—alone. He has no sense. He does not know anything about our country."

Then the Dreamer gave a stirring sermon on the Creator, the mother, and the homelands they could never leave. Joseph and the other chiefs pulled their blankets over their shoulders to show their agreement. The warriors, their blood rising, rumbled in accord with Grating Sound's strong words.

A few treaty Nez Perce, moving about the crowd, were spying on their non-treaty cousins on behalf of the army. They looked and listened for signs of a violent uprising and feared that Grating Sound's defiant speech might trigger one.

Frances Monteith, the grown daughter of the translator Perrin Whitman, later said, "If we were to be massacred, we would all go together. And it looked as though we might, more times than once."

Howard quickly called for a weekend break, worried about the red-hot mood of the warriors.

The following Monday, Grating Sound spoke strongly again of the Creator, the mother, the land . . .

Howard angrily cut him off. All that Dreamer talk was beside the point, he said. He repeated his order that all Nez Perce would move to the reservation, or he would put them there by force.

Grating Sound shouted, "Who are you to tell me what to do?"

"I am that man," Howard answered.

"I am chief here!" Grating Sound cried. "No one can come and tell me anything I must do. I am a man. You will not tell me what to do."

Howard was a battle-hardened general. People followed his commands, period. He had the stubborn, defiant chief arrested for disobeying the president's order to relocate. Grating

Sound was locked up, stripped, and dressed in a prisoner's white nightshirt.

Howard's threats alone were insulting. But arresting a respected chief? And making him wear what the Nez Perce considered women's clothing? This was an outrage!

Joseph's nephew, a twenty-one-year-old warrior named He-me-ne Mox-mox (Yellow Wolf), would later say, "All that hurt us. In peace councils, force must not be talked [threatened]. It was the same as showing us the rifle."

The general believed he was keeping an unruly man in line and making clear to the others that he was in charge. Not fully understanding Nez Perce culture, he had no idea that "showing the rifle" would have the opposite effect. Grating Sound's

The warrior Yellow Wolf posed with a rifle in his left hand and a tomahawk, or war club, in his right hand for this photograph, c. 1909.

General Oliver Otis Howard (1830–1909)

General O. O. Howard was born on a farm in Maine. Though a graduate of West Point, the army's officer training academy, he thought about being a preacher. When the Civil War broke out in 1861, he commanded Union troops at some of the bloodiest battles: Fair Oaks (where he lost his arm), Bull Run, Antietam, Gettysburg, and others. He even joined Sherman's March to the Sea, a cruel and ruthless attack designed to destroy the South once and for all. After the war, the leader of that attack, General William Tecumseh Sherman, became head of the U.S. Army in Washington, D.C.

Howard helped found a school in 1866 to train teachers and preachers of all races and both genders. He taught religion at what was later named Howard University. Then, in the 1870s, he joined the Indian wars in the West. His boss, General Sherman, wrote in a letter, "The more [Indians] we can kill this year, the less will have to be killed the next war."

Howard worked out a surrender treaty with Cochise, a Chokonen fighter who had fought both Mexicans and Americans in the Southwest. Then, in his late forties, he was appointed to the Northwest region, which included the Nez Perce and other groups.

In 1908, the year of this photo, General Howard published *Famous Indian Chiefs I Have Known*. His book features Joseph, Cochise, Geronimo, Sitting Bull, and other famous Native Americans.

warriors cried for war. They would never forget or forgive this terrible insult.

Peace at Any Cost

Joseph did everything in his power to calm the warriors. He argued that the Nez Perce could easily kill all the soldiers present, but then many more troops would arrive. Soldiers would blame all the traditional bands, even the women and children, for the deaths, and kill many Nez Perce in revenge. In the end, they would lose their land anyway, just like the Cayuse.

Yellow Wolf, Joseph's nephew, would later explain: "None of the chiefs wanted war. . . . No chief talked or wanted war. . . . I am telling you three times, no chief wanted war." Three times meant the Wallowa warrior was not speaking with two tongues.

The warriors seethed but backed down—for now.

Joseph would later say, "If I had said nothing, General Howard would not have been alive to give an unjust order against my men."

For a couple days, Joseph, Looking Glass, White Bird, and others rode with Howard around the Lapwai reservation. The general kept pointing out land where the Nez Perce bands could settle. Joseph still intended to keep his homeland. He treated the reservation tour as a chance to sway Howard toward that end. Through a translator, the men chatted like friends.

As Howard softened, the chiefs asked for the release of Grating Sound. The general agreed but still stuck fast to his primary order. Back at council, he announced that the Nez Perce had thirty days to move their people, their horses and cattle, their tepees—everything!—to the reservation. Period.

Joseph tried to stall for time, clinging to the hope that he could find a way to keep his land. He pointed out that it was spring, a time of melting snow and heavy rains. The swollen rivers were too dangerous for their cattle to cross.

The general refused. End of council.

Joseph, Frog, and their warriors made the long journey back up the mountains to Wallowa. To their shock, they found soldiers already posted there, right next to the Nez Perce women and children. True to Howard's word, the soldiers had orders to remove the Wallowa band by force, if necessary.

Joseph would later explain his painful choice: "I did not want my people killed. I did not want anybody killed. I said in my heart that rather than have war, I would give up my country."

He decided to leave his land, and the bones of his father, to save his people's lives. Sadly, quickly, the band began packing.

On June 12, 1877, two days before Howard's deadline, about seven hundred Nez Perce from several bands camped at Camas Prairie, Idaho, not far from the reservation. Camas Prairie was named for its rich supply of camas roots—a

He decided to leave his land, and the bones of his father, to save his people's lives.

staple of the Nez Perce diet. While camped there, the women and girls dug up as many roots as they could to dry and store them for food. Young boys played games and raced horses. The older people gambled, smoked tobacco, and told stories. More than a hundred warriors staged a parade, beating their shields and whooping it up.

Sergeant Michael McCarthy wrote in his diary, "Quiet peace reigns. Joseph has put pride in his pocket. . . . White Bird . . . is present at our morning drills nearly every day."

Missing from this gathering was Chief Looking Glass's band. The chief stopped by to tell the other chiefs that he had chosen not to move. He thought that he could keep clear of settlers, avoid

A Charles Russell painting (c. 1892) captures the breakneck need for speed during a horse race. Young Nez Perce boys raced horses while waiting at Camas Prairie.

trouble, and the *so-ya-pu* would leave him alone. Unlike the other bands, his people had taken up farming, and they wanted to harvest their crops. Looking Glass then returned to his village at the edge of the reservation.

A Warrior's Revenge

During this time, Joseph and Frog set out from camp with a small group to kill some of their cattle for meat. They had left the animals behind because the herd couldn't cross the swollen river without drowning. Upon returning to Camas Prairie on June 14, they were surprised to find that all the other bands except theirs had cleared out.

A warrior told them both happy and crushing news. Joseph's second wife, To-ma Al-wa-win-mee (Springtime), had given birth to a daughter. Meanwhile, three warriors had triggered a bloody killing spree. Their leader was Wah-lit-its (Shore Crossing). His father had been murdered in 1875 by a *so-ya-pu* named Larry Ott. Ott was still free—just like the killers of Wind Blowing.

The three warriors had fumed over this injustice and the humiliating arrest of Chief Grating Sound. They couldn't find Ott, so they rode from cabin to cabin, killing other innocent settlers. Husbands were shot dead in front of their terrified wives. A few of the women and a child were also attacked—acts that went against Nez Perce honor. The three rampaging warriors brought stolen guns and whiskey back to the Camas Prairie camp. They got drunk and rallied others to join them—including Chief Grating Sound himself. The large group of raiders set out to kill again.

Joseph sank with grief at the news. He would later say, "I would have given my own life if I could have undone the killing of white men by my people."

He knew what these murders meant. His people were now at war with the United States of America.

CHAPTER 6

The War of 1877

I had counseled peace from the beginning. I knew we were too weak to fight the United States. We had many grievances [complaints], but I knew that war would bring more.

Soldiers would be coming—this was certain. The bands of Joseph, Grating Sound, and White Bird hid inside White Bird Canyon, south of the Idaho reservation. This steep-walled crack in the earth, near the Idaho-Oregon border, was part of Chief White Bird's homeland.

Joseph held out hope that he could talk his way out of an attack. He wanted to explain to General Howard that a

At Fort Lapwai, chiefs Joseph, White Bird, and Looking Glass gathered their men for this photo about a month before the War of 1877 broke out.

small group of warriors had acted on their own and that the chiefs still wanted peace.

A Nez Perce scout spotted troops at dawn on June 17, 1877. Six warriors rode out of camp to meet them. The lead rider held a white flag of truce, a symbol that meant "Hold your fire!" Ignoring it, Ad Chapman and other volunteer fighters who hated the Nez Perce fired the first shots. The War of 1877 had begun.

Back at the White Bird Canyon camp, Joseph led the effort to move people as far away from the battle as possible. The boys rushed to herd the horses, which were grazing a distance away. The women and girls packed up their tepees and belongings.

Frog rode out toward the battle site, wearing his chief's sash. White Bird and Grating Sound roused their warriors. Many of the men were still sleeping off the previous night's drunken raids and did not stir.

Yellow Wolf and other more clear-headed fighters took aim at the soldiers from hidden positions in the hills. A

A wood engraving shows Nez Perce warriors driving their horse herd away from attackers during the War of 1877.

sharp-shooting warrior killed the **bugler** from more than a thousand feet away. The warriors knew that without a bugler, the captain could no longer broadcast his orders to his troops. Next, warriors tried to pick off the officers. In a top-down chain of command, this strategy was like cutting off the heads of snakes.

Besides Chapman, other volunteers fought beside the troops. These men were farmers and ranchers and had no chance against skilled warriors. Most of them fled back to their homesteads. Even the professional soldiers were poorly trained and rusty shooters due to their lack of target practice. Their horses were not used to battle and shied at the sound of gunshots. Many of the soldiers cowered or scattered, unable to hold their positions for more than five or ten minutes.

The Nez Perce warriors forced a retreat in less than an hour and then returned to their families. They chose not to slaughter a group of pinned down *so-ya-pu*, who they could hear crying in fear and pain.

Though outnumbered two to one, not a single Nez Perce was killed. Thirty-four soldiers lost their lives.

Outrunning the Cavalry

The warriors rejoiced, but Joseph knew this fight was far from over. The chiefs held a quick council to discuss their options. Stay and fight was not one of them. General Howard would come after them with more and better troops and powerful weapons. Also, the local settlers were out to kill the Nez Perce for murdering their relatives and neighbors.

Surrender? Never, said White Bird and Grating Sound. They would all be hanged for murder, just like the Cayuse who were blamed for the Whitman massacre.

Joseph realized, with a heavy heart, that the time for talking was over for good. He let the older war chiefs take the lead.

Retreat was the only choice, the group decided. Yet how could families, with children and elderly people, outrun the U.S. cavalry? Where would they go?

The warriors rejoiced, but Joseph knew this fight was far from over.

The chiefs decided to cross the raging Salmon River to the west. As migrants, the Nez Perce were experts at this difficult feat, using buffalo skins as boats. The U.S. Army, with its heavy cannons and wagons and lack of know-how, would have to cut logs and build rafts. That extra time would give the retreating Nez Perce a head start.

Warriors stayed behind to taunt the troops into crossing from the opposite bank. Among the soldiers, they spotted James Reuben, now the leader of the Christian Nez Perce. He was scouting for the army against his own people! The warriors shouted: "You are getting fat eating government food! . . . Come and get us! . . . We will take your scalps!"

The taunts worked. As the troops labored to cross the Salmon River, the Nez Perce recrossed the waterway at

James Reuben shouted, "You cowardly people!" at the warriors across the river. He believed they were being too proud to listen to reason and that their pride cost too many lives.

This June 2008 photo shows the Clearwater River near Lapwai, Idaho. As in June 1877, spring rains have swelled the water

another point. When enemy scouts approached on the opposite bank, the warriors again taunted them.

To follow the Nez Perce, the troops now had to recross the Salmon River. They had left their raft at the site of the first crossing. So they took apart the log cabin of a Christian Nez Perce scout and made a new one.

Hundreds of Nez Perce, even with their teeming horse herd and all their belongings, outpaced the soldiers for a couple of weeks. In early July, they camped on the Clearwater River, north of the Salmon River and southeast of the Lapwai reservation.

Soon, an enraged Looking Glass joined them. He told them he had posted a white flag of truce at his village. Because his band was innocent of all murders, he thought he had nothing to fear.

By contrast, General Howard, through clouded eyes, saw the non-treaty Indians as one people—Joseph's people. Stevens and Hale had made the same mistake at the treaty councils. On July 1, 1877, the general ordered soldiers to burn Looking Glass's village to the ground. Local settlers stole all the band's horses and cattle.

Looking Glass declared, "Now, my people, as long as I live I will never make peace with the Americans. I am ready for war."

Attack at Clearwater

On the morning of July 11, 1877, the first four Nez Perce to die in the War of 1877 were about to fall. The army launched a surprise attack on the Clearwater campsite. All day, Nez Perce women brought fresh horses and ammunition to the fighting warriors. On the second day, most of the warriors began trickling back to camp. Unlike soldiers, who obeyed a commander, the Nez Perce were free to fight or not as they pleased. Now, many of them chose to retreat rather than risk their lives.

Yellow Wolf and a warrior named Wot-to-len (Hair Combed Over Eyes) suddenly realized they were fighting alone. They were the last to withdraw as bullets whizzed past them, and the big howitzer cannon boomed behind them.

As he retreated, Yellow Wolf spotted Joseph's wife, Springtime, on a bucking horse. She couldn't mount the skittish horse while carrying her child, so her newborn baby was on the ground, strapped to a **cradleboard**. Yellow Wolf quickly picked up and handed the baby to Springtime, and they raced to catch up to the retreating band.

Joseph was leading that band. He was helping families head for the hills in a hasty panic. They left behind cooking pots full of food, their supply of camas roots, tepee poles, buffalo skins, and

A baby had no chance to escape or fall out—or even move very much —while in a cradleboard (c. 1899).

other items. Among the remains, looting settlers found an old woman in her nineties, alive but too weak to travel.

Days later, the chiefs sent Howard a message that they were ready to surrender to the army. It was a false offer, meant to stall the general. The trick worked. Howard waited, in vain, for Chief Joseph to show up and lay down his weapon.

The massive Nez Perce group used this head start to make their way north in Idaho. They camped at a forest clearing called Weippe Prairie, which had plenty of water and grass for the horses. This was the same spot where explorer William Clark had met three Nee-mee-pu boys in 1805. In fact, Clark had fathered a

A Teenager's View of the Battle

Ee-lah-wee-mah (About Asleep) was a fourteen-year-old member of Chief Joseph's band during the War of 1877. He and his younger brother carried water to the warriors, including their father. Here, About Asleep describes what he saw from a rifle pit at the Battle of Clearwater.

"A lot of warriors were there. . . . I got in this walled-up hollow and after a time raised up and looked across to where the soldiers were. They fired the big gun [a cannon] many times. I got scared. . . . When the cannon-guns [boomed], rocks were showered and limbs of trees cut down. Smoke from that gun was like grass on fire. . . . I jumped out from there and ran! Soldiers must have fired at me, for bullets sang by but none touched me. Reaching for my horse, . . . I sprang on him and made for camp. . . . [Soldiers] began firing across the river among our tepees. . . . The Indians were now running their horses for the mouth of the canyon, leaving most of the tepees and other material. No time to save only a part of the camp. It was wild hurrying for [the] shelter of the canyon hills. . . . One of those big cannon-guns sent a ball into the air. . . . Soldiers were firing just as often as they could, and I saw my horse was stopped from running. . . . [It] was shot through the left shoulder. . . . [My brother-in-law] gave me a horse he was leading. I pulled the saddle from my crippled [horse] and threw it on this new one. . . . We were soon in the hills where their shots could not reach us."

The "big gun" described above was probably a howitzer cannon, such as the one shown in this 1862 Civil War image. A Nez Perce warrior named Peopeo Tholekt (Bird Alighting) captured a howitzer in battle, but couldn't budge it. He took off the gun and wheels and buried them to disable the powerful weapon.

Nez Perce son named Daytime Smoke. That son, now age seventy-one, was among the fleeing Nez Perce band.

Weippe Prairie was just east of the Lapwai reservation, but most of the treaty Nez Perce at Lapwai wanted nothing to do with their hunted cousins. The non-treaty Nez Perce had killed too many white men. Many Christian Nez Perce, in addition to James Reuben, were actively scouting for the army. Family against family! A brother of the warrior Yellow Wolf was caught spying for the army. Two Christian Nez Perce named Captain John and Old George had daughters in the non-treaty group. Hoping to retrieve them, the two men would follow the retreat to the end, scouting all the way for General Howard.

Where Next?

At council, Chiefs Looking Glass and Grating Sound discussed settling in buffalo country—on the plains of Montana. There, they had trading and hunting partners among the Flathead and Crow

The Crow (above) and the Nez Perce had a common enemy—the Blackfeet. The two allies hunted, traded, and held councils together. Until the fall of 1877, their friendship was solid.

peoples. Even *so-ya-pu* merchants would help them along the way, Looking Glass said. A long-time buffalo hunter, he knew some of them like brothers.

Chief White Bird suggested going north to Canada to join Sitting Bull and his Lakota people. Like the Lakota who killed Custer's cavalry last summer, the Nez Perce would be beyond the reach of the U.S. Army there. The problem was that they would have to cross the land of the Blackfeet, one of their worst Native American enemies.

Chief Joseph spoke from his heart. He asked, now that they were at war, what were they fighting for? Their lives? No. They were fighting for the land where the bones of their fathers were buried. That's where they should die. He longed to leave the women and children of his band in a mountain hideaway and return to the Wallowa River valley to face the soldiers. Joseph wouldn't get his way. He was a peace chief, and the Nez Perce were at war. The strong words of Looking Glass now carried more weight.

On July 16, 1877, Chief Looking Glass took charge of the long, miserable retreat over the Bitterroot Mountains into Montana. Joseph knew his band couldn't risk traveling alone. So he decided, with a heavy heart, to join the retreat.

They were fighting for the land where the bones of their fathers were buried.

Looking Glass chose to cross the jagged border between Idaho and Montana by way of the Lolo Trail. This buffalo-hunting path followed the high, less forested ridgeline of the mountains. It was easier for horses to walk than the bushy foot trails below. Even so, the Lolo Trail was extremely steep, narrow, and winding in places. General William Tecumseh Sherman, commander of the

A newspaper illustrated the 1877 pursuit of "Joseph's people." The army camp and its rising smoke are visible far in the distance across the Montana plain.

U.S. Army, called it "one of the worst trails for man and beast on this continent." With some eight hundred people and a couple thousand horses, the retreating group stretched out over five miles.

Looking Glass thought that, once Idaho was behind them, they could take their time and regroup. He believed they had no quarrel with the soldiers and settlers of Montana. He was also certain that General Howard wouldn't pursue them beyond his Northwest Territory.

What the chief failed to understand was that, unlike the Nez Perce, the *so-ya-pu* were united under a single leader. Howard received stark orders from General Sherman in Washington, D.C.

He was to pursue the fleeing Nez Perce to the death.

CHAPTER 7

On the Trail to Montana

We understood that there was to be no further war.
We intended to go peaceably to the buffalo country.

Despite General Sherman's orders, Howard didn't chase Joseph's people—his term for the whole Nez Perce band—right away. He didn't know which way they were headed. The mountains of Idaho were crisscrossed with hundreds of trails, and the migrant Nez Perce knew them well. In addition, in the wake of the killings, terrified settlers were begging the soldiers to stay and protect them. So, Howard called in more troops and waited for them to arrive at Fort Lapwai.

Meanwhile, his Native American scouts searched the wilderness for signs of the fleeing Nez Perce. The fact that such a massive group of people and horses could move undetected gives some idea of just how vast that wilderness was.

For eleven grueling days, the Nez Perce trudged over the Lolo Trail in the Bitterroot Mountains. While Chief Looking Glass was in the lead, Joseph's band trailed at the back of the pack. The Wallowas slogged through the muck and breathed the dust of thousands of feet trampling ahead of them, both human and horse. The trail was littered with rocks and fallen trees, which made walking slow, tough, and tiring for everyone. Having lost all their tepee poles at the Battle of Clearwater, the families slept under rock ledges and piles of brush at night.

Scouts constantly searched the trail behind the group for signs of soldiers. They found none. Still, Looking Glass didn't dare slow down while they were still in General Howard's Northwest Territory.

Safe Passage in Montana

On July 25, 1877, the Nez Perce finally crossed through the Lolo Pass from Idaho into Montana. The U.S Army was building Fort Missoula, Montana, an army outpost near the border. Looking Glass, Joseph, and the other chiefs met with the local commander, Captain Charles Rawn. They hoped to cross the land peacefully, but armed warriors stood nearby—just in case.

In the summer of 1877, the building of Fort Missoula had just begun. Fort Missoula, pictured here, is now a museum.

Looking Glass's heart sank when he spotted about twenty Flathead warriors among Rawn's two hundred troops and volunteer fighters. His buffalo-hunting friends had sided with the *so-ya-pu*! The Flathead warriors wore white arm and headbands so as not to be mistaken for Nez Perce if a fight broke out. Their chief, Charlos, told Looking Glass that the Nez Perce had blood on their hands, and his hands were clean. He wanted no part of their war.

Captain Rawn demanded that the Nez Perce give up their guns. If they did, he promised he would not attack or arrest them. They could travel through western Montana unharmed.

Looking Glass flatly refused. His people would keep their guns, but he promised the captain that they would not kill or rob anyone as they passed through. Looking Glass added that he only fought when there was no other choice.

Captain Rawn wisely agreed to let the group go—guns and all. Outnumbered, the last thing he wanted was to provoke the desperate Nez Perce into attacking. Besides, he knew that far larger forces were on the way. General Howard had sent orders for Rawn to delay the group as long as possible to give his troops time to catch up. Also, Colonel John Gibbon, head of Fort Shaw, was leading his troops along the Blackfoot River in Montana toward the fleeing Nez Perce. Fort Shaw was about six days' travel to the northeast of Fort Missoula.

Looking Glass led the Nez Perce south, along the Montana-Idaho border, toward a buffalo hunter's camp in Montana called Big Hole. Word of the Idaho murders had reached the entire Bitterroot River valley, and the local *so-ya-pu* locked their doors in fear. Some two hundred and fifty women and children huddled for three weeks inside Fort Owen, a crumbling trading post near the town of Stevensville. Other families quickly pieced together small forts out of slabs of sod.

Colonel John Gibbon (1827–1896) joined the North in the Civil War, despite being from North Carolina. He spent the rest of his career fighting Native Americans in the Plains states.

On the first day of August, more than a hundred finely dressed Nez Perce warriors paraded down the main street of Stevensville, a town of less than two hundred people. They were looking for items to buy. The stores were shuttered and emptied of their goods. Only a few merchants, like the owners of the Buck Brothers General Store, saw fortune where others saw danger. They cautiously opened for business.

As the Nez Perce shopped, Chief White Bird kept an eagle-eyed watch over the warriors, especially Grating Sound's hot-blooded bunch. A single bad act could trigger an all-out battle.

Imagine looking out of a tiny, paned window at hundreds of well-armed, colorfully dressed Nez Perce on horses. This historic cabin still stands in Stevensville, Montana.

Henry Buck observed about the Nez Perce, "Never shall I forget their . . . stern looks, their aggressiveness, and their actions, which . . . placed us immediately on the defensive. This added . . . to our present fear and left a life-long impression." Yet he also called the Nez Perce "by far the finest looking tribe of Indians I have ever seen," with showy new blankets, the latest Henry rifles, and excellent horses.

The Bucks and other people who dared to trade with the group became instantly rich. Thanks to those excellent horses, the Nez Perce were one of the wealthiest peoples in the Northwest. They bought a huge stash of food and supplies to replace what they had lost at Clearwater. They paid in gold and silver coins and paper money that the women hid in their long, thick braids. In just two days, the group spent about a thousand dollars—equal to about $20,000 in today's money.

The Best Horses in the West

In 1806, explorer Meriwether Lewis with the Corps of Discovery noted that the Nee-mee-pu had the largest horse herd on the continent. He wrote, "Their horses appear to be of an excellent race; they are lofty, elegantly formed, active, and durable."

As migrants, the Nez Perce relied heavily on horses for travel, hunting, war, and trade. Their strong, sturdy, sure-footed horses could carry people and belongings along steep mountain trails. Their war and hunting horses were fast and agile with short manes and tails so as not to get caught on brush.

Above all, the Nez Perce became famous for favoring eye-popping patterns. They developed horse breeds that were pied, or spotted, like the Appaloosa and Pinto. The colors and patterns of their coats were like paintings: leopard-like spots, splashes of snowflakes, marble-like speckles, tiny white dots like a fine frost on a dark coat, and ink-like splotches on a white coat.

By breeding the best horses in the West, the Nez Perce became rich. Their high-quality stock also helped them outpace the cavalry during the long retreat of 1877. Afterward, their stolen herd would be dispersed. The fine breeding would be watered down through mating with horses of lower quality.

A modern-day Nez Perce man donned traditional clothing and posed on a "painted pony"—the nickname for an Appaloosa horse.

Rest or Run?

The Nez Perce crossed the **Continental Divide** and traveled down the eastern face of the Bitterroot Mountains onto rolling meadows. On August 7, after fleeing for seven weeks over hundreds of miles, Looking Glass decided to stop and rest at Big Hole. This well-known campsite near the Idaho border had plenty of grazing grass and a freshwater creek. Looking Glass wanted to give the women time to make tepee poles for the rest of the long journey.

Chief White Bird and many of the warriors were uneasy with this decision. Peo-peo Ip-se-wak (Lone Bird) cried, "My shaking heart tells me trouble and death will overtake us if we [don't] hurry through this land! . . . Let's [go] to the buffalo country!"

Hair Combed Over Eyes had dreamed about everyone being killed. So did Shore Crossing, the warrior whose killing spree had triggered this war.

Looking Glass dismissed these fears. The war was over, he told them. Assured by their safe passage and friendly trading in Stevensville, he was certain all their troubles were behind them.

> *"My shaking heart tells me trouble and death will overtake us if we [don't] hurry through this land!"*

He also wanted to rest the horses. The Nez Perce still had hundreds of miles to travel to reach the plains.

Yellow Wolf felt uneasy and wanted to scout for troops, just to be sure. The young warrior would later complain, "Looking Glass was against everything not first thought of by himself."

Joseph said nothing. Heartsick, he was losing hope of ever returning to Wallowa as the band traveled farther and farther

Heyoom Yoyikt (Bear Crossing) was Chief Joseph's older wife and the mother of Noise of Running Feet. Chief Joseph would wed four women and father nine children in his lifetime.

away. As camp chief, the best he could do was make sure the horses and families were healthy and well fed. He was also caring for two wives, each with a daughter, one twelve years old and the other an infant.

The next day, his wives and the other women cut and scraped logs to make tepee poles—twelve poles per lodge. The *chop-chop-chop* echoed into the hills near the campsite. By evening, under Joseph's direction, the band had set up eighty-nine buffalo skin tepees in a double, V-shaped row.

Hunters brought back an elk and some trout, which the women cooked. Though exhausted, people stayed up late, eating, singing and dancing to drums, playing games, and telling stories. They were counting on getting their first good sleep in almost two months.

They had no idea of the tragedy that was about to strike.

CHAPTER 8

To Kill or Be Kind?

We could have killed a great many women and children while the war lasted, but we would feel ashamed to do so cowardly an act.

At three o'clock on the morning of August 9, as the Nez Perce soundly slept, a single shot rang out in the darkness. Then four more shots. Then the rapid *pop-pop-pop-pop* of Gatling guns. That sound was followed by the clamor of soldiers and volunteer fighters, more than two hundred strong, charging on horses through the camp.

Bullets ripped through the animal skin walls of the tepees. The soldiers aimed low, hoping to kill as many

The Gatling gun, invented in 1861, had six barrels. Soldiers rotated them with a hand crank to shoot rounds quickly, one after the other. This 1870s model fired 200 bullets per minute.

sleeping people as they could. They set fire to lodges with families still inside them. They killed babies and sick people and old people who weren't able to run.

The groggy sleepers were slow to react.

Yellow Wolf, who shared his uncle Joseph's tepee, said, "I was half sleeping. I lay with eyes closed. Maybe I was dreaming? I did not think what to do!"

Tired and confused, he and the other warriors searched for their weapons in the darkness. They had no time to wonder who was shooting at them.

Women and children scrambled to safety like frightened mice. Boys and girls hid under blankets in their tepees or ran with their mothers to a nearby creek. Many who fled were chased down and shot in the back.

Joseph, unarmed, scooped up his baby daughter and hid by the creek while his brother Frog rallied the Wallowa warriors.

White Bird shouted at his stumbling men, "Brave men fight for their women and children! It is better that we die fighting!" His warriors were the first to spring into action.

Joseph, unarmed, scooped up his baby daughter and hid by the creek . . .

Looking Glass told Shore Crossing, "I would rather see you killed than the rest. You started this war. Now fight!"

Shore Crossing kept firing his rifle up to the moment when soldiers swarmed down and killed him. His pregnant wife picked up the rifle and shot a soldier before being shot to death herself.

As the dawn sun showed its face, about ten sharp-shooting warriors drove the enemy across the creek and into the hills. They still weren't sure who these soldiers were or where they had come from. In any case, they realized, their retreating enemies had no safe place to hide on the grassy meadow.

The warriors pinned down the soldiers with gunfire, giving the families a small window of time to retreat. Joseph and the boys rushed to herd the horses. Nez Perce women and children returned to the scorched camp to discover dead sons and daughters, sister and brothers, wives and husbands, mothers and fathers. The soldiers and warriors, just a few hundred yards away, heard the survivors wail, long and loud, with grief and horror.

The Nez Perce had little time to mourn. Joseph helped families bury their dead in quick graves and strap their wounded kin onto tepee poles. Then the group fled south, away from the soldiers and the bloody Big Hole killing field.

The U.S. army lost the Battle of Big Hole. Warriors drove the soldiers away. But this haunting memorial in western Montana reminds visitors of the terrible loss of life among the Nez Perce.

A Widening Net of Soldiers

After reaching a safe distance, Joseph led the hasty effort to set up camp, made more difficult by broken hearts and spirits. Warriors trickled in to join their bands. From the fighters, Joseph learned that their attacker wasn't General Howard. The warriors had cornered a volunteer fighter, who told them the general was still two days behind. Who could these new enemy soldiers be?

Like Howard, Colonel John Gibbon, the head of Fort Shaw, had orders from General Sherman to stop the runaway Nez Perce at all costs. After leaving Fort Shaw, he had joined Captain Rawn at Fort Missoula. The two officers recruited some one hundred and fifty volunteer fighters among the settlers. Heading south, hot on the Nez Perce's trail, they followed the *chop-chop-chop* of the tepee pole makers to the Big Hole camp.

How did army officers from far-flung forts track down the Nez Perce over hundreds of miles? They had a form of instant messaging called the telegraph. The telegraph allowed the general, the colonel, and the captain to communicate quickly with one another and to receive orders from General Sherman in Washington, D.C.

Joseph and the other chiefs took a death toll. They counted eighty-nine people dead, including some of their best warriors. Most of the dead were the elderly, children, and women, including Frog's wife. Joseph was shocked and angry at the cruelty. Killing innocents was the act of a coward, not a brave. One soldier had smashed in the mouth of a young girl! Another had crushed the head of a newborn and shot the mother! In one tepee, the surviving Nez Perce found five children, all killed.

How could any human being be so heartless? Joseph had no answer.

Instant Messaging in the Old West

An American named Samuel Morse sent the first instant message by telegraph in 1838, two years before Chief Joseph was born. An operator tapped out a dot-and-dash code for letters and words on the machine. The coded signals zipped along electrical wires to another machine. A second operator translated the code back into letters and words. All this can take place in seconds, even if the machines are in different cities and states.

By 1877, at the dawn of the telephone era, telegraph wires were humming coast to coast in the United States. General Howard in Idaho received instant orders from General Sherman in Washington, D.C. Howard sent messages to Captain Rawn and Colonel Gibbon in Montana, well ahead of his arrival. Two other commanders, Colonel Samuel Sturgis and Colonel Nelson Miles, would join the pursuit. These five units, all under the command of General Sherman a couple thousand miles away, coordinated a fifteen-hundred-mile chase across three states.

More than the rapid-fire Gatling gun, more than the big, booming howitzers, the telegraph was the army's most powerful weapon.

By contrast, the non-treaty Nez Perce sent oral messages by way of men riding fast horses. News could take days or weeks to pass from one band to another.

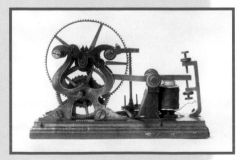

On May 24, 1844, Samuel Morse sent his first message across official telegraph lines using this hand-built machine. By 1877, telegraph wires crisscrossed the vast continental United States.

Custer's gravestone stands in the tall grass at the Little Bighorn National Monument in Montana, where Custer and members of the 7th Cavalry fell in 1876.

What the chief did not know was that the previous summer, Gibbon's unit had been at the Battle of the Little Bighorn. He and his troops arrived a day too late to save Custer's cavalry unit. Instead, their sad task was to identify and bury the hacked-up bodies of their fellow soldiers. At Big Hole, many of these men were out for revenge. They didn't care that Nez Perce had nothing to do with the Little Bighorn massacre. To them, an Indian was an Indian.

From his returning warriors, Joseph learned another shocking fact. Some of those volunteer fighters at the Big Hole massacre were the traders and merchants from Stevensville.

The warrior Yellow Wolf would later say, "These citizen soldiers! Good friends in Bitterroot Valley! Traded with us for our gold! Their Lolo peace treaty was a lie! Our words were good. They had two tongues."

A New Leader

At the next council, the chiefs blamed Looking Glass for the massacre. After all, it was his decision to stop at Big Hole to rest. It was his decision not to send out scouts. He was the one who boldly told them that the war was over.

Joseph again talked of returning to the Wallowa River valley and fighting for his homeland—to the death, if necessary. Again, his words carried little weight.

White Bird and Grating Sound agreed that a subchief named Wah-wook-ya Wa-sa-aw (Lean Elk) should lead the group rather than Looking Glass. The Nez Perce could not afford to get lost while on the run, and this short, loud-spoken buffalo hunter knew Montana well. Lean Elk also spoke a little English.

Buffalo country was to the east. But Lean Elk set a speedy, roundabout course to the southeast to avoid Montana towns such as Helena and Virginia City. Tepee poles were now out of the question. They were too heavy to carry while moving fast. Families slept under animal skin tarps hung over branches.

Part of Joseph's job as camp chief was to aid grieving family members and to comfort them in their pain and guilt. Everyone felt crushed each time the quick pace forced people to leave behind wounded, old, and sick relatives. They gave their loved ones a blanket, water, and food, but death was certain. It often came at the cruel hands of Howard's Bannock scouts. The fierce Bannock people lived in southwestern Montana. Many scouted and fought beside U.S. soldiers, sometimes shocking the troops by killing and scalping old and wounded Nez Perce.

To slow the soldiers, Frog and Grating Sound decided to lead a raiding party. On the night of August 20, they and their warriors snuck up on General Howard's men at Camas Meadows, two days behind the Nez Perce camp. In the darkness, they stole his pack mules, thinking they were horses. Even so, without animals to carry supplies, Howard fell several more days behind.

Three groups of warriors set out each day to search for signs of troops in all directions. The attack at Big Hole had cost most of their food and supplies, so they raided ranches and farms. They

This 1878 wood engraving preserves the sorrowful faces of a starving Bannock band. After an uprising that year, General Howard chased down hundreds of Bannock. The captives were imprisoned.

killed *so ya pu* men to keep them from reporting the group's location to the army. To Joseph's dismay, some warriors spoke of wanting to kill all *so-ya-pu*—women too!—in revenge for the Big Hole massacre.

The Nez Perce didn't know it, but news of these killings zipped across the country by telegraph and newspaper. In the eyes of the nation, these "wild Indians" were on the warpath—out to kill as many whites as they could.

Taking Innocent Prisoners

Thanks to Lean Elk's quick pace, the group crossed from Montana into Wyoming and arrived at Yellowstone Park in late August. Founded in 1872, Yellowstone was the nation's first national park. Five years later, this public land was still mostly raw wilderness.

Spectacular sights, such as the famous Old Faithful geyser, still draw streams of tourists to Yellowstone Park. Sky-high jets of water erupt when underground steam builds up pressure.

From the start, Yellowstone was famous for its spectacular shooting geysers, colorful springs, and burping mud pots. These natural wonders drew a few hundred hardy tourists each summer. Roving groups of Nez Perce warriors stumbled on these happy campers like wolves on sheep. At best, they stole their food and supplies. At worst, they killed them, partly for revenge and partly to keep them from reporting the Nez Perce location. Some warriors, especially those in Grating Sound's band, were cruel and violent. Others acted with honor.

On August 24, 1877, Yellow Wolf's group returned to camp with three *so-ya-pu*, a woman, a man, and a teenaged girl. Warriors taunted and whooped at the captives to scare them.

Yellow Wolf told Joseph that the other seven members of the *so-ya-pu* group had been shot or escaped. Joseph grew angry at his nephew. Every death, every theft, every abuse of innocent people fueled hatred in the hearts of settlers toward the Nez Perce. These crimes also helped justify the war in the minds of the U.S. soldiers. Why would Yellow Wolf take innocent tourists prisoner?

The young warrior explained that it was the tourists' idea. They asked specifically to see Chief Joseph! He had no idea how these strangers, so far from Wallowa, knew his uncle's name.

The warriors in his scouting party were of two minds. Some wanted to kill the tourists. Others did not. Yellow Wolf thought it best to let his uncle decide.

Showing Acts of Kindness

Joseph had no intention of harming these innocent people— just the opposite. He welcomed the two *so-ya-pu* women into his humble lodge—a simple buffalo skin tarp. Lean Elk hosted the man, Frank Carpenter.

Emma Cowan, twenty-four years old and newly married, wore a long skirt with buttoned shoes. As she shivered in the autumn cold, her freckled face tensed with fear. To calm the *so-ya-pu* guest, a woman in the lodge handed her a Nez Perce baby. Holding the infant put the new wife at ease. Cowan later wrote that this tender moment was the only time she saw Chief Joseph smile. She described him as somber, serious, and silent.

The War of 1877 left a deep and permanent sorrow on the face of Chief Joseph, as shown in this photo from 1903.

The other female captive was Ida Carpenter, the thirteen-year-old sister of Frank. She later wrote, "The squaws [women] soon had supper, and gave me some bread and tea made of willow-bark. The tea was so bitter I could not drink it. . . . They made my bed on some buffalo robes, and the squaws laid down all around me, and thus watched me until morning."

Ida and Emma didn't eat much during the few days they spent with the Nez Perce. But both captives said later that their captors were very kind to them the entire time. They were even given moccasins to replace their worn-out shoes. Joseph relied on these acts of kindness and Lean Elk's broken English to spread a message of peace.

In his loud, booming voice, Lean Elk asked the *so-ya-pu* to tell their friends that the Nez Perce wanted no more war. He repeated his fractured message so many times that Emma became annoyed. To her, bullets spoke louder than words. During the raid on their camp, warriors had shot her husband, George Cowan, in the head, hip, and leg. She thought he was dead, though she would later learn that he had barely survived.

At council, the chiefs decided to release their prisoners unharmed. The next morning, as families packed up camp, Joseph gave the three *so-ya-pu* food, moccasins, matches, blankets, and two slow horses to carry them to Bozeman, Montana, some forty miles away. The woman and girl could ride, Lean Elk said, but the man had to walk. He didn't want them to give away the camp's location too soon.

> . . . *Lean Elk asked the* so-ya-pu *to tell their friends that the Nez Perce wanted no more war.*

Joseph would later say, "They were treated kindly. The women were not insulted. Can the white soldiers tell me of one time when Indian women were taken prisoners, and held three days and then released without being insulted?"

Old Woman Land

The group crossed from Wyoming back into Montana, heading northeast toward Crow country. They camped near the spectacular Mammoth Hot Springs, a white and yellow cascade of stone, and then exited Yellowstone Park. After meeting with the Crow, Looking Glass discovered that his buffalo hunting friends had taken the army's side. Like the Flathead, the Crow didn't want the powerful United States as an enemy.

Mammoth Hot Springs is located near the Wyoming-Montana border. The colorful rock terraces have changed since 1877. They constantly reform as groundwater deposits minerals and bacteria.

Despite Joseph's kindness toward the tourists, the Nez Perce had too much blood on their hands. Settling safely in Montana was now out of the question.

At council, Joseph brought up the idea of surrender. Day after day, he cared for people who were cold, hungry, tired, and sick. If they didn't die on the trail, he argued, they would die when soldiers finally caught up and attacked again. By turning themselves in, Joseph said, they could save lives.

White Bird and Grating Sound flatly refused. Looking Glass was of the same mind: "I have my experiences with a man of two faces and two tongues. If you surrender, you will be sorry, and in your sorrow, you will feel . . . dead."

The war chiefs decided the only safe place to go was north, to Old Woman Land. The "old woman" was Queen Victoria, the royal figurehead of Canada. The border was about four hundred miles away, perhaps a three-week journey. Looking Glass hoped the Lakota exiles in Canada—Sitting Bull's people—would be more sympathetic than his Flathead and Crow "friends."

Lean Elk continued to drive the exhausted group, roughly seven hundred in number, at a brutal pace. While they traveled due north in September, temperatures dropped below freezing at night. All day, their large herd of horses kicked up clouds of dust that could be seen for miles on the treeless plains. The Nez Perce had no place to hide.

The long retreat was now a desperate race for the Canadian border through enemy territory.

CHAPTER 9

Attack at Bear Paw

With a prayer to the Great Spirit, I dashed unarmed through the line of soldiers. It seemed to me that there were guns on every side. My clothes were cut to pieces . . . but I was not hurt.

At the end of September 1877, as a storm rolled overhead, the Nez Perce reached Bear Paw in northern Montana. In all, starting from their camp back at Camas Prairie, Idaho, they had traveled roughly fifteen hundred miles. Now, three-and-a-half months later, they were only two suns—two days' travel—from Old Woman Land.

Scouts reported that Howard was many suns behind them. They had nicknamed him General Day-After-Tomorrow for lagging two days behind during the retreat. Now, he was even farther away.

Chief Looking Glass rode through the Nez Perce camp, telling families to rest. The

The Nez Perce Retreat, 1877

CANADA

WASHINGTON

Lapwai Reservation
Clearwater R.
Blackfoot R.
Lolo Pass
Fort Missoula
Fort Shaw
Bear Paw
Missouri R.

Battle of Clearwater
Battle of Whitebird Canyon
Looking Glass's village
BITTERROOT MTS.
MONTANA
Battle of Big Hole
Fort Keogh

OREGON
Salmon R.
Snake R.
IDAHO
Yellowstone National Park
Crow Reservation

WYOMING

Sitting Bull's camp

0   100 MI
0   200 KM

···· Route traveled by Nez Perce
······ Route traveled by Colonel Miles

How did hundreds of ailing men, women, and children outpace five units of American soldiers? The U.S. military regarded the 1,500-mile retreat as one of history's most amazing feats.

outspoken leader was now trail boss again. Lean Elk's fast-paced march had made too many people tired and sick.

The boys took the large horse herd across Snake Creek to graze. Thanks to a recent warrior raid on a large *so-ya-pu* supply station, the families were now flush with supplies. Hunters also provided the group with fresh buffalo meat. With hills on three sides of the camp, the families lit fires without fear of being spotted. Joseph was relieved to see that hot food and a nearby promised land revived the weary travelers.

The next morning, September 30, was cold and windy with rain turning into snow. A few families gathered their horses and packed early. Looking Glass, Joseph, and others took their time to gain some much-needed rest. Most people were still eating breakfast when two scouts raced into camp. They had spotted a cloud of dust on the plains. They reported that soldiers were on their way.

Looking Glass didn't believe it. He thought it was the dust of a buffalo stampede, nothing more. There was no way General Day-After-Tomorrow could catch up so quickly. The chief urged families, "Do not hurry! Go slow! There's plenty, plenty time. Let children eat all they want!"

About an hour later, a scout on a hill signaled that the enemy was attacking—now!

The Cavalry Charge

A dozen or so families that were already packed took off north across the snowy plain just ahead of the attack. They would make it safely to Canada.

Warriors stripped for battle, grabbed their rifles, and ran to positions of defense on the hills. Over the crest, they spotted cavalry and foot soldiers charging in two wide columns. The

Soldiers charged at the Nez Perce (far left) with better weapons and far greater numbers of fighters. The man on the right with the white hat and sword is an officer—making him a primary target of the warriors.

soldiers were moving to surround the Nez Perce and cut them off from the horse herd. Soldiers charged at full speed toward the camp, guns firing.

Yellow Wolf would later say, "You have seen hail, sometimes, leveling the grass. Indians were so leveled by the bullet hail." To his horror, he spotted Cheyenne warriors in long-feathered war bonnets and stripped for battle. They were leading the charge! Yellow Wolf feared these skilled warriors more than the soldiers and aimed to kill them first.

Meanwhile, Joseph and others ran to save the horses. Most of the herd was scattered. His daughter Noise of Running Feet managed to catch and mount one of the frightened horses and ride for her life toward Canada. So did fourteen-year-old About Asleep, About Asleep's younger brother, and a few other Nez Perce. Chief Joseph thought of Springtime and his infant daughter and raced to find them.

"With a prayer to the Great Spirit," the chief later said, "I dashed unarmed through the line of soldiers [toward camp]. It seemed to me that there were guns on every side. My clothes were cut to pieces, and my horse was wounded, but I was not hurt."

The peace chief grabbed a rifle from Springtime and fought. "Six of my men were killed in one spot near me," he later said. "We fought [the soldiers] at close range, not more than twenty steps apart."

Though outnumbered, the Nez Perce warriors killed enough attackers—one out of five!—to force a retreat. After targeting the Cheyenne, they killed or wounded three captains, a lieutenant, and all the first sergeants. The leaderless soldiers fell back and circled the camp—like a noose.

A Standoff

That evening, with the enemy at bay for now, the chiefs took stock of their losses. The army had captured or scattered most of the horse herd. To Joseph's lifelong grief, his brother Frog had died in the attack, as did Chief Grating Sound, along with five or six warriors by his side. In the fast, frenzy of battle, Chief Lean Elk and three top warriors were mistakenly killed by their own people.

As night fell, the chiefs sent scouts through the soldiers' line under the cover of darkness. The messengers headed north to contact Sitting Bull in Canada. With the horse herd lost and General Howard on the way, the best hope was for the Lakota warriors to come to their rescue. For now, Joseph told people to hunker down and wait.

While the men were fighting, the women had dug pits in the hillsides, using pots and sticks and knives. They would make

Hand-dug earth shelters protected the women and children from bullets but not from the booming howitzer shells. They risked their lives to collect drinking water from a stream.

about a hundred of these earth shelters by the end of the battle. All day, they hid inside with their children, wet and shivering.

On the second morning, October 1, soldiers and warriors continued to trade taunts and bullets. The battle became a siege— a standoff that could only end badly for the Nez Perce.

Chief Joseph received a message demanding that he surrender. The Nez Perce were confused. Why was the message directed to Joseph? White Bird was the older chief. Looking Glass was the trail boss. It did not matter. The sender's name was what interested Joseph. Their new enemy was a man named Colonel Nelson Miles.

Like Howard and Gibbon, Miles had received orders from General Sherman to stop the Nez Perce at all costs. The officers guessed, correctly, that the group would try to flee the country.

A Nez Perce Woman Remembers

The stories of the Nez Perce women and children in the War of 1877 are often overlooked. Historians tend to focus instead on chiefs and warriors, weapons and battles, and military strategy.

A Nez Perce woman, her name unknown, gave this description of the Bear Paw battle: "We dug the trenches with camas hooks and butcher knives. With pans, we threw out the dirt. We could not do much cooking. Dried meat and some other grub [food] would be handed around. If not enough for all, it would be given [to] the children first. I was three days without food. During the last fight, I heard many make the remark, 'I have not eaten since we were attacked!' Children cried with hunger and cold. Old people suffered in silence. Misery everywhere! Cold and dampness all around!

"In the small creek was water, but we could get it only at night. In traveling, we had buffalo horns for [getting] water. With strings, we could let them down while crossing streams on horseback. We carried them with us all the time. They came in handy here [at Bear Paw]."

The colonel had marched his troops about 150 miles from the southeast toward the Canadian border.

Colonel Miles fought under General Howard in the Civil War. But he hoped to capture the Nez Perce before his former commander arrived at Bear Paw. A big victory over "hostile Indians" would help Miles rise to the rank of general. So far, he had failed, but the colonel knew the Nez Perce were trapped.

The young chief replied to Miles by messenger that he would not surrender, but he was open to talking. Words were

President Theodore Roosevelt called the tall, handsome Nelson Miles (1839–1925) a brave peacock. Nelson rose quickly to commander of the U.S. Army in 1895. Marrying General Sherman's niece probably helped.

Joseph's strong point. He wanted to hear what this *so-ya-pu* leader was thinking.

A False Truce

The two men met halfway between the camps under a white flag, each leader backed by his top men. Miles noted the bullet holes in the chief's striped blanket, buckskin top, and leggings. When he asked again for a surrender, Joseph did not say yes. Though no agreement was made, they shook hands. Joseph turned to go back to camp. Then the colonel committed an act that was unthinkable to the Nez Perce. He took the chief prisoner, just as Howard had arrested Chief Grating Sound at council the previous May.

The November 1877 issue of *Harper's Weekly* magazine told the story of the Battle of Bear Paw in a series of pictures. Above, a Nez Perce warrior raises a white flag to signal surrender.

"That white flag was a lie!" cried Yellow Wolf, outraged. He blamed the arrest of Grating Sound for starting this war. Now, his own chief, his uncle, was a prisoner!

Miles ordered Joseph to be tied up and wrapped in a blanket so that he couldn't move. The chief slept among the mules, as a storm covered the battlefield in snow.

The Nez Perce snatched a soldier, a lieutenant, in return. They gave the officer food and a blanket. The next day, in a prisoner exchange, Miles let Joseph return to camp. Then he sent Old George and Captain John to talk the chief into surrendering.

The two Christian Nez Perce scouts were thrilled to find their daughters still alive. Hoping to take their children safely back to Lapwai, they urged the chiefs to give up. White Bird, Looking Glass, and Joseph all refused.

For the next three snowy days, the Nez Perce families hid in the earth pits. The army shelled the camp with its deafening howitzer, blasting craters in the ground. One of the exploding shells made a direct hit on a shelter pit, killing a girl and her grandmother and wounding four others, including a small boy.

Soldiers and warriors fired at one another from hidden positions. No one was killed until a warrior pointed at a small cloud of dust on the plains. Chief Looking Glass stood up to see if Lakota warriors were coming to the rescue. He took a bullet in his forehead and died instantly. The dust cloud turned out to be a Nez Perce warrior.

The death of Looking Glass meant that White Bird, the elderly warrior, and Joseph, the voice of peace, were the last non-treaty Nez Perce chiefs alive.

Escape or Surrender?

On the night of October 4, the fifth day of the battle, General Howard and his troops arrived. White Bird, Joseph, and the warriors held a council. Fighting meant certain death, they agreed. Fewer than a hundred warriors couldn't possibly stand up to six hundred soldiers. And they couldn't count on the Lakota to help them. They had no way of knowing if their messengers made it to Canada.

What about surrender? Colonel Miles had promised Joseph that the band could stay in Montana for the winter. Then, in spring, they could return to the reservation at Lapwai and live in peace. They could even keep the horse herd, he assured them.

White Bird angrily dismissed any thought of turning himself over to the *so-ya-pu*. He said the Nez Perce could never trust the word of a white man. He felt certain they would be killed or, at best, put in prison. He chose to escape—or die trying. Anyone who was willing and able could go with him to Canada, slipping through the soldiers' line at night. Almost all of the warriors, including Yellow Wolf, agreed to join him.

Fewer than a hundred warriors couldn't possibly stand up to six hundred soldiers.

Joseph said, "I do not wish to leave our wounded, I do not wish to leave the bodies of our dead unburied here in this hollow. I do not want to see the blood of our children reddening the snow."

The Wallowa chief decided to give up the fight.

Around two o'clock in the afternoon on October 5, Chief Joseph gave one of the most famous speeches in American history. He poured out his "sick and sad" heart to Colonel Miles and

In a glorified illustration, the Nez Perce give up their rifles. Joseph called this dramatic moment an end to the war, as agreed by both sides. History records it as a surrender.

Chief Joseph's Famous Speech

Chief Joseph's speech was translated and passed through several messengers. So, it is likely that these are not his exact words. Still, his raw emotion on that tragic day rings true and clear.

"I am tired of fighting. Our chiefs are killed. Looking Glass is dead. Too-hool-hool-zote is dead. The old men are all dead. It is the young men who say yes or no. He who led the young men [Frog] is dead.

"It is cold, and we have no blankets. The little children are freezing to death. My people, some of them, have run away to the hills and have no blankets, no food; no one knows where they are—perhaps freezing to death. I want to have time to look for my children and see how many of them I can find. Maybe I shall find them among the dead.

"Hear me, my chiefs. I am tired. My heart is sick and sad. From where the sun now stands, I will fight no more forever."

General Howard. Ad Chapman, one of the volunteer fighters who had fired the first shots of the War of 1877, translated the Nee-mee-pu words into English. A reporter wrote down the speech, no doubt adding his own flourish.

Chief Joseph's speech ended with the famous line, "From where the sun now stands, I will fight no more forever."

CHAPTER 10

Fame from Misfortune

Let me be a free man—free to travel, free to stop, free to work, free to trade where I choose . . . free to follow the religion of my fathers, free to think and talk and act for myself.

As many as one hundred fifty Nez Perce died in the War of 1877, either in battle or along the trail. Roughly two hundred thirty people escaped to Canada, many of them led by White Bird.

On October 5, 1877, the rest of Joseph's people became prisoners of war under guard by the U.S. Army. These captives weren't warriors who raided and killed settlers and troops. They were mostly the old, the sick, the wounded people, and others who could flee no farther. They would eventually number four hundred thirty-one, after some escapees were rounded up. They included one hundred seventy-eight women and almost the same number of children.

Colonel Miles promised that the prisoners would be well cared for. He told Joseph, "No more battles and blood! From this sun, we will have good times on both sides, your band and mine. We will have plenty of time for sleep, for good rest."

To Joseph's great relief, the colonel kept this promise. As camp chief, Joseph had looked after these weary, grieving people for three-and-a-half months. He was

Nelson Miles lived in the officer's quarters (above) of Fort Keogh, which was closed in 1889. The vast, treeless range is now a cattle ranch in Custer County, Montana. Nearby Miles City was named after the colonel.

heartbroken over the loss of his brother Frog and so many other family members. Finally, they could all sleep soundly, no longer afraid of being attacked at any moment. They rested, ate, and regained some strength. The army doctor treated their injuries and ailments.

Colonel Miles prepared to lead Joseph's band to his home base, Fort Keogh, Montana, on the Yellowstone River. Their winter camp would be under his watchful eye.

Joseph still believed that Nez Perce and *so-ya-pu* could someday live peacefully together. He had turned General Howard into an admirer during their first meeting. Now, he set out to sway this new foe, Colonel Miles, to his side. Joseph softened Miles with heartfelt words. As the thirty-seven-year-old chief and the thirty-eight-year-old colonel led the Nez Perce band south across the plains, the chief spilled out his sad tale. He told the story of the thief treaty of 1863 . . . the killers who went free . . . Howard's showing of the rifle at Fort Lapwai . . . the killing of women and children and old people at Big Hole.

Over the two-week trek, the colonel came to respect, admire, and sympathize with Joseph. Joseph even won over the hardheaded translator, Ad Chapman. Colonel Miles would spend the rest of his life trying to help Joseph's people. Because of their newfound respect, Joseph never blamed Miles for what happened next. White Bird turned out to be right: The *so-ya-pu* government could not be trusted.

The Long Journey Continues

Joseph, Miles, and the Nez Perce band arrived at Fort Keogh on October 23, 1877. Just six days later, the colonel received orders to move the Nez Perce prisoners east, to Fort Lincoln at Bismarck, North Dakota. The army wanted to keep them as far from Sitting Bull's defiant band as they could. Also, the government could shelter and feed the prisoners more cheaply at a fort closer to a city.

Joseph's heavy heart dropped yet another rung at the news. His homeland was to the west, not the east. His people had just traveled two thousand miles, most of it on the run. Now, sick and feeble, with winter near, they had to travel four hundred miles more to some strange place?

Miles was upset, too. He tried but failed to convince his commander to let the Nez Perce recover in Montana and then go to Lapwai, as he had promised Joseph. He explained to Joseph, "The chief who is over me has given the order, and I must obey it or resign. That would do you no good. Some other officer would carry out the order."

Joseph knew that Miles was speaking the truth. He walked from lodge to lodge and gently, softly told his people to get ready for yet another long journey.

Adding salt to the wound, Joseph learned that the group would be traveling without their prized horse herd. The Cheyenne, Bannock, and Crow who fought for the army had already received about one hundred and fifty horses as payment. The army kept some, too. About one hundred animals died on the trail from Bear Paw to the winter camp. It's unclear what happened to the others, along with dozens of fine saddles.

Joseph's heavy heart dropped yet another rung at the news. His homeland was to the west, not the east.

Joseph would later lament, "We gave up all our horses, over eleven hundred, . . . and we have not heard of them since. Somebody has our horses."

Without their horses, the Nez Perce were transported by so-ya-pu means. For most of them, this was a scary, first-time experience. The strongest

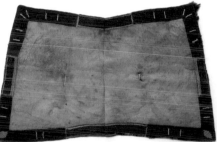

Chief Joseph's saddle blanket, made of buffalo hide, is at the Buffalo Bill Historical Center in Cody, Wyoming.

people traveled overland in horse-drawn wagons. The weaker ones boarded fourteen boats and sailed on the Yellowstone River. As the river travelers arrived at Fort Lincoln, they heard two booming cannon blasts, a piercing train whistle, and the scream of steam from a locomotive's engine. Having never seen a train before, the Nez Perce flattened themselves on the decks of the boats in fear. They didn't know that the cannon fire was a signal to the boats to stop for inspection.

The Northern Pacific Railway put Bismarck on the map in 1873 by building a railroad station there (above). When Joseph arrived in Bismarck, he was surprised that many citizens knew who he was.

Those traveling by wagon soon arrived, led by Miles and Joseph. At a small fort along the way, Joseph had given a speech to hundreds of Native Americans. Not sharing a common language, he gave the entire talk in sign language, without speaking a word. The crowd understood him perfectly as he told his long, sad tale of how the Nez Perce became prisoners of the U.S. Army.

Upon arriving in the noisy city of Bismarck—the biggest they had ever seen—the Nez Perce were allowed to shop using the little gold and cash that was left over from their spree in Stevensville. The shop owners marveled at their exotic new customers.

Joseph's Story

Joseph was also stunned to discover that, among the *so-ya-pu*, he was famous. Everywhere Joseph went, crowds of citizens gawked at the great Chief Joseph. They cheered and waved at him. Reporters begged for interviews. Then they wrote exaggerated accounts of his heroic role in one of the greatest military retreats in American history. The published articles added to Joseph's fame. Few people of the day understood that much of this fame was based on myth rather than facts.

Joseph's fame explained why the tourists at Yellowstone knew his name. It also explained why Miles had addressed his surrender

A September 1877 issue of *Harper's Weekly* promoted the false image of Joseph as a warrior. Compare this artist's view with photos of the real Chief Joseph in this book.

Separating Myth from Fact

History has shown that Chief Joseph was a great leader who cared deeply about his homeland and his people. He was neither a noble hero nor a monster. To set the record straight, here are the facts of his role in the War of 1877.

Myth	Fact
The Nez Perce were Joseph's band.	The group had several independent bands, only one of which was Joseph's.
Joseph attacked a white woman during the killing spree that triggered the war.	A man of peace, Joseph was nowhere near the place of the attack.
Joseph led one of the longest, most brilliant retreats in military history.	Looking Glass and Lean Elk led the retreat. Joseph was the camp chief.
Joseph was an unjust tyrant, bent on conquering the West.	Joseph repeatedly said he only wanted to live peacefully on his land in the traditional way.
Joseph was a noble warrior, fighting white injustice with bullets.	Joseph fought injustice with words, not weapons.

In 1878, a year after the war, artist Cyrenius Hall softened the public image of Chief Joseph by choosing rich, warm earth tones for this painting.

message to Joseph and not White Bird or Looking Glass. Joseph still did not understand how or why he was famous. Even so, he quickly understood that he could use that fame to help his people. With the support of the public, maybe the Nez Perce could even return to their land.

That evening, the city of Bismarck put on a fancy dinner party in honor of Colonel Miles—the man credited with capturing the Nez Perce. Instead of a tale of military glory, Miles talked sincerely about the injustices suffered by Joseph's people. He spoke of the chief's great leadership skills and tender caretaking of suffering families. The townspeople were moved.

The next evening, the town threw a second banquet—this time in honor of Chief Joseph. The quiet, dignified chief wore moccasins with fancy stitching. His white, beaded necklace was wrapped many times around his neck to form a cascade of bands.

Showy earrings, bright white beads, and thick, black braids could not mask the grief etched in Chief Joseph's face. The death of so many Wallowas, including his brother Frog, weighed heavily on his mind.

His leather shirt, though bullet-ridden, sported patterns of colorful beads. A red chief's sash worn around his waist completed the ornate outfit.

Chief Joseph told his story, with Chapman serving as translator. He would repeat versions of the epic tale every chance he got for the rest of his life.

His opening statement was usually a plea for understanding: "I want the white people to understand my people," he said. "Some of you think an Indian is like a wild animal. This is a great mistake. I will tell you all about our people, and then you can judge whether an Indian is a man or not."

Then he recounted the history of his people and white people, starting with the warm friendship of Lewis and Clark. He talked of renewing that friendship between the two peoples. Finally, he made a simple request to live free and peacefully on the land of his father's bones.

People applauded and cheered.

The Hot Place

Shockingly, the long journey still wasn't over. In Bismarck, Miles broke the heavy news to Chief Joseph that General Sherman decided to send the trail-weary prisoners south, to a jail in Fort Leavenworth, Kansas.

"When will these white chiefs begin to tell the truth?" Joseph wondered aloud, within earshot of a reporter.

Sherman's attitude was harsh: "These Indians are prisoners, and their wishes should not be consulted." Still, he denied a request by the Idaho settlers to hang thirty-one Nez Perce as murderers, including Chief Joseph.

Joseph and his people traveled to Kansas by train—a loud, scary, bone-shattering journey for these expert horse riders. At

The prison at Fort Leavenworth, opened in 1875, had gated windows and guard towers The thick walls were suffocating to a people used to camping and migrating across wilderness land.

stops along the way, fawning fans greeted the famous Joseph warmly. A group of 418 prisoners arrived on November 27, 1877. Living in a disease-infested prison took a terrible toll. About twenty Nez Perce soon died, including newborns—mostly from a disease called malaria. Still, Joseph continued to provide interviews and to give his speech about peace, friendship, and freedom.

The following year, during the scorching summer of 1878, the government forced the prisoners to move yet again —from Kansas to Oklahoma. There, they would join other Native Americans on reservations. The plan was to convert these migrant Nez Perce into farmers, as their Christian cousins had done at Lapwai. If successful, they would need fewer government handouts.

The *so-ya-pu* called this flat, windswept land Indian Territory. The Nez Perce named it Eekish Pah (the Hot Place). They arrived

Land reserved for Native Americans was often too dry and barren to grow crops. This photo shows an early twentieth-century Cheyenne village in Oklahoma.

at the Hot Place tired, grieving, and unable to bear the hot, dry climate. They had no horses or cattle, no lodges, and no more gold dust or cash. Once a rich, independent people, they now lived on government money. To make matters worse, the government agent in charge stole most of their allotment and did little to help them.

Meeting the President

Joseph rode his fame to the highest level. On January 17, 1879, President Rutherford Hayes agreed to meet, briefly, with the celebrated chief in Washington, D.C. This was the first in a series of meetings with U.S. presidents over the next few decades. In front of senators and congressmen and other *so-ya-pu* leaders, Joseph gave a stirring speech. He pleaded that his people be allowed to return to Wallowa, or at least to Lapwai.

He said, "What I have to say will come straight from my heart, and I will speak with a straight tongue. The Great Spirit is looking at me, and will hear me. . . . I believe much trouble and blood would be saved if we opened our hearts more. . . . We only ask an even chance to live as other men live. . . . Let me be a free man—free to travel, free to stop, free to work, free to trade where I choose, free to choose my own teachers, free to follow the religion of my fathers, free to think and talk and act for myself."

President Rutherford B. Hayes (1822–1893) supported efforts to strip Native American children of their language and culture and convert them to a wholly white lifestyle.

The crowd stood and clapped and whistled. Even so, his words brought no relief. At the Hot Place, his people continued to die, their numbers plummeting to fewer than three hundred. Even the government agents began to fear that Joseph's band might become extinct.

Daytime Smoke, the son of William Clark, was one of the many Nez Perce to die. Joseph's baby daughter, name unknown, was another victim. She was born just a couple days before that first battle, at White Creek Canyon. Her entire, brief life consisted of war, prison, sickness, and then death.

Joseph thought of his daughter Noise of Running Feet, who had fled on horseback at the battle at Bear Paw. Was she alive? Was she well? Was her *wayakin* still protecting her?

Return to the Northwest

By the 1880s, the Nez Perce, like most Native Americans, were confined to reservations—like cattle, as White Bird once said. James Reuben was now the leader of the Lapwai Reservation. He led other Christian Nez Perce to plead for the return of their cousins to the northwest. He rallied Presbyterians across the country to write letters and provide aid. Reuben also succeeded in converting some of Joseph's band to Christianity.

In 1883, the U.S. government finally agreed that twenty-nine war widows and children could move to Lapwai, Idaho. Two years later, the remaining Nez Perce prisoners were allowed to resettle on two reservations. One was Lapwai, where the Nez Perce would have to live in houses on small plots of land and become Christians. One hundred and eighteen Nez Perce chose that course, under Reuben's leadership. The other option was Colville, a wilderness in northern Washington near the Canadian border. There, the Nez Perce could live as they pleased. Joseph

A Reservation Report

John Scott, a government agent in charge of the Nez Perce, filed yearly reports. His sole measure of success was how well the tribe adapted to white ways. However, like many of the other agents, he came to favor returning them to the Northwest. The following is an excerpt from a report.

"These Indians are in some respects superior to those of any other tribe connected with the agency. They are unusually bright and intelligent; nearly one-half of them are consistent members of the Presbyterian Church. . . . The entire band, with perhaps one or two exceptions, are quiet, peaceable, and orderly people. They receive what is provided for them with apparent thankfulness, ask for nothing more and give no trouble whatever. They are extremely anxious to return to their own country. They regard themselves as exiles. The climate does not seem to agree with them, many of them have died, and there is a tinge of [sadness] in their bearing and conversation that is truly pathetic. I think they should be sent back [to Idaho], as it seems clear they will never take root and prosper in this locality . . ."

and about one hundred and fifty followers chose Colville in May 1885.

Living among his own people, Joseph went by his *wayakin* name, Thunder Rising Over Distant Mountains. He married a couple of war widows and lived with them in a tepee, turning down a government house. Though he wore some western

Residents of the Colville Reservation (c. 1910) dressed in their traditional best for a dance.

clothing, he kept his white beaded necklace, the feather headdress, his chief's sash, and his colorful moccasins.

Still trading on his fame, he gave speeches all over the country. He never stopped his fight to return to the Wallowa River valley, the land of his father's bones.

CHAPTER 11

A Broken Heart

I have a kind feeling in my heart for all of you.

Chief Joseph never saw his only surviving child again. He had last seen his daughter, Noise of Running Feet, galloping away from the battle of Bear Paw in 1877. He heard that the girl had made it to Sitting Bull's camp in Canada. After spending the winter there, she returned to Montana with a group led by Yellow Wolf. But the killings of the previous summer were still fresh on people's minds, and the Nez Perce were not welcomed there.

Noise of Running Feet surrendered, and the government allowed her to move to Lapwai. In 1879, she married a Christian Nez Perce and changed her name to Sarah Moses. She sent a photograph of herself to her father at Colville and died, childless, a few years later.

Yellow Wolf, too, eventually surrendered. As he rode through the Nez Perce homeland, he was overcome with sadness. "The places through which I was riding came to my heart," he said. "It drew memories of old times of my friends, when they were living on this river. My friends, my brothers, my sisters! All were gone! No tepees anywhere along the river. I was alone."

The young warrior chose to settle at Colville with his uncle. He raised two sons there and lived to around the age of seventy. He told his story in a book shortly before dying in 1935.

The Bones of the Father

In June 1900, a government agent took Joseph and a few of his people on a short trip to the Wallowa River valley. It was the turn of the twentieth century, the Modern Era. The Northwest territories were all U.S. states now, peppered with towns and cities and saw mills and churches. Rails and roads and telephone wires crisscrossed the mountains and valleys. The Indian wars were long over. The Wild West was now a road show featuring Buffalo Bill Cody. Joseph had even seen the show and was treated like a celebrity.

Almost sixty years old, the chief visited the graves of his mother and father on the Wallowa River. A caring settler had built a fence around them. Joseph wept bitterly as he placed a fresh horsehide over the spot where their bones were buried.

Buffalo Bill Cody (far right) turned the cowboys and Indians of the old Wild West into a traveling show. He paid Joseph, Sitting Bull, Geronimo, and other chiefs to appear in his show.

Joseph's people stayed in this long house on the Colville Reservation, far from their traditional winter camp in the Imnaha River valley. The woman standing in front is unknown.

He said, "I love that land more than all the rest of the world. A man who would not love his father's grave is worse than a wild animal."

Later, vandals would rip into the earth and steal the skull of Tu-eka-kas. In 1926, the remains were moved to Wallowa Lake.

Joseph and the agent met with the local citizens in a Wallowa town called Enterprise. He had a few friends in the large crowd, but most of the locals still treated him like a murderer. With war a fading memory, and a new generation born, the chief hoped those people would soften. If they did, maybe they would allow him to return to his land. He even told the agent he was willing to buy his people's land—even though he had never sold it.

In the Nez Perce language, Chief Joseph told his story yet again. He asked to reclaim the land where his parents were buried in the Wallowa Lake area, as well as the winter camp and long

Here, near Wallowa Lake, lie the bones of Chief Tu-eka-kas—minus his skull, which was stolen. His monument begins the Nez Perce National Historic Trail, a 1,500-mile road trip that retraces the famous 1877 retreat.

house at the Imnaha River valley. As his words were translated into English, the crowd laughed. Those places were prime settlement areas! To them, the idea of giving up valuable tracts of land was absurd.

In his report, the agent recommended that Chief Joseph remain at Colville. He reasoned that the settlers deserved to keep the land because they had built ranches and towns and churches and schools on it.

A Kind Heart

Joseph never gave up his promise to his father to fight for Wallowa. In 1903, he met with his last U.S. president, Theodore Roosevelt. They cordially ate buffalo together, but Joseph's plea for his land fell on deaf ears.

The chief also met his old foe, General Howard. Joseph spoke of how he once wanted to kill this enemy. Then he said, "Ever

Theodore Roosevelt (1858–1919) wrote that taking the land of "savages"—by treaty or war—was just and good for civilization. Joseph had no chance of swaying the hardheaded president.

This ticket entitled a "lady and gentleman" to hear Chief Joseph speak at the Seattle Theater.

since the war, I have made up my mind to be friendly to the whites and to everybody. . . . I have no grievance against any of the white people, General Howard or anyone."

Then, in November, he traveled to Seattle, Washington, to give what turned out to be his last public speech. The discovery of gold at Colville had, once again, triggered a rush of settlers onto Nez Perce land. Nonetheless, he told the crowd of *so-ya-pu*, "I have a kind feeling in my heart for all of you." Then he told his story one last time.

Back at Colville, Joseph stoked the fire in front of his tepee early one morning and sat before it. The aging chief had a broad belly, sunken shoulders, and bowed legs. His deep, black eyes looked sad and mournful.

A painting of Chief Joseph exaggerates his death, just as a nation exaggerated his life.

Where Are the Nez Perce Today?

Today, many of the descendants of both the treaty and non-treaty bands live on reservations at Lapwai, Colville, and in Canada. Others left the reservations to live wherever they pleased in other parts of the country.

What happened to the survivors of the War of 1877? The aging chief White Bird made it to Canada and remained there with Sitting Bull. In 1892, he was killed in a dispute with one of his own men. A daughter of Looking Glass, renamed Martha Mintorn, lived to the age of ninety-three. She died in 1949 in Lapwai, Idaho, after having spent part of her life in Canada.

About Asleep, the fourteen-year-old boy who, like Joseph's daughter, had escaped to Canada at the Battle of Bear Paw, survived the war. After Joseph died without any heirs, About Asleep became chief of Joseph's band at the Colville Reservation.

About eight o'clock on September 21, 1904, one of his wives went to get him for breakfast. She found him slumped over, dead.

A *so-ya-pu* doctor wrote that Chief Joseph died of grief. Joseph's kind heart was broken. But his message of peace lives on in these powerful words: "Whenever the white man treats the Indian as they treat each other, then we will have no more wars. We shall all be alike—brothers of one father and one mother, with one sky above us, and one country around us, and one government for all. Then the Great Spirit Chief who rules above will smile upon this land, and send rain to wash out the bloody spots made by brothers' hands from the face of the earth. For this time, the Indian race are waiting and praying. I hope . . . that all people may be one people."

Glossary

acquitted—found to be not guilty in a court of law.

baptized—formally made a member of and believer in a church.

boomtowns—towns that became rich quickly and grew fast as a result.

bugler—soldier who plays a bugle (small trumpet) to sound out a commander's orders in battle.

cavalry—soldiers trained to fight on horseback. Today's cavalry ride in trucks and helicopters.

commission—a group appointed by a person in charge to carry out a specific task.

Continental Divide—a mountain ridge where the rivers of a continent on either side of the mountain travel in opposite directions.

cradleboard—a wooden carrier for babies that could be strapped to a mother's back or a horse.

economic—having to do with goods, services, and money.

migrants—people who move from one region to another, often with the seasons.

mission—an outpost in a remote area built to spread a religious faith. Missions usually include a church, a school, and a home for missionaries.

prophets—religious leaders who are believed to foresee the future or speak the will of God.

ratify—to formally approve, usually by a majority vote. Once a treaty is ratified by Congress, its provisions are carried out.

reservation—land reserved, or set aside, for a group of people.

scalp—remove the skin and hair from the top of an enemy's head as a trophy.

shaman—in Native American culture, a healer and seer of the future who is believed to be in touch with the spiritual world.

tepees—shelters made of wooden poles arranged in a cone, with the pointed tip at the top and a waterproof cover such as animal skins or canvas.

treaty—a formal agreement between peoples or nations.

vision quest—a spiritual ritual common to many Native American peoples in which an individual seeks guidance or knowledge by entering into trance. The trance is induced by starvation, lack of sleep, and/or natural chemicals.

Bibliography

Books

Beal, Merrill D. *"I Will Fight No More Forever."* Seattle and London: University of Washington Press, 1963.

Cash Cash [sic], Phil. *The Poetics of Nii-Mii-Puu (Nez Perce) Naming.* University of Arizona, 2005.

Chief Joseph. *That All People May Be One People, Send Rain to Wash the Face of the Earth.* Kooskia, Idaho: Mountain Meadow Press, 1995.

Greene, Jerome A. *Nez Perce Summer 1877: The U.S. Army and the Nee-Me-Poo Crisis.* Helena: Montana Historical Society Press, 2000.

Hampton, Bruce. *Children of Grace.* New York: Henry Holt, 1994.

Howard, O. O. et al. *In Pursuit of the Nez Perces.* Kooskia, Idaho: Mountain Meadow Press, 1993.

Josephy, Alvin M. *The Nez Perce Indians and the Opening of the Northwest.* New Haven and London: Yale University Press, 1965.

McWhorter, L. V. *Hear Me, My Chiefs! Nez Perce Legend and History.* Caldwell, Idaho: Caxton Printers, 2001.

———. *Yellow Wolf: His Own Story.* Caldwell, Idaho: Caxton Printers, 1986.

Nerburn, Kent. *Chief Joseph and the Flight of the Nez Perce.* San Francisco: Harper, 2005.

Stadius, Martin. *Dreamers: On the Trail of the Nez Perce.* Caldwell, Idaho: Caxton Press, 1999.

Wifong, Cheryl. *Following the Nez Perce Trail.* Corvallis, Oregon State University Press, 2006.

Articles and Letters

Buck, Amos. "Review of the Battle of the Big Hole": *Montana Historical Society Contributions*, 1910.

Chief Joseph. Speech at Carlisle Industrial School (March 1904).

Huggins, E. L. "Smohalla, the Prophet of Priest Rapids": *Overland Monthly* 17, January–June, 1891.

Sherman, General William Tecumseh. "Letter to John Sherman" (September 23, 1868).

Web sites

Lewis, Meriwether, and Clark, William. *The Journals of Lewis and Clark.* http://lewisandclarkjournals.unl.edu

McDermott, John Dishon. *Forlorn Hope: A Study of the Battle of White Bird Canyon Idaho.* National Park Service, 1968. The entire text is posted online at http://www.nps.gov/archive/nepe/shs/.

Source Notes

The following list identifies the sources of the quoted material found in this book. The first and last few words of each quotation are cited, followed by the source. Complete information on each source can be found in the Bibliography.

Abbreviations

AP—*That All People May Be One People, Send Rain to Wash the Face of the Earth*
BB—*Review of the Battle of the Big Hole*
CG—*Children of Grace*
CJ—*Chief Joseph and the Flight of the Nez Perce*
DR—*Dreamers: On the Trail of the Nez Perce*
GS—*General Sherman's letter to John Sherman*
HM—*Hear Me, My Chiefs!*
IP—*In Pursuit of the Nez Perces*

LC—*The Journals of Lewis and Clark*
NP—*Following the Nez Perce Trail*
OM—*Overland Monthly*
SP—*Speech at Carlisle Industrial School*
YW—*Yellow Wolf: His Own Story*

INTRODUCTION: War or Peace?
    PAGE 1 *"If the white man . . . need be no trouble."*: AP, p. 85
    PAGE 1 *"Horses! Save the horses!"*: YW, p. 205
    PAGE 1 *"Fight!"*: AP, p. 65

CHAPTER 1: A Boy with a Heavy Load
    PAGE 2 *"I have carried . . . since I was a boy."*: AP, p. 29
    PAGE 6 *"all had eyes like dead fish."*: CJ, p. 4
    PAGE 6 *"great confusion"*: CJ, Sept. 20, 1805
    PAGE 6 *"signs of fear."*: CJ, Sept. 20, 1805

CHAPTER 2: Speaking With Two Tongues
    PAGE 15 *"[Our fathers] told us . . . speak the truth."*: AP, p. 3

CHAPTER 3: A People Divided
    PAGE 25 *"I learned then . . . was large."*: AP, p. 29
    PAGE 29 *"My young men . . . in dreams."*: OM
    PAGE 30 *"Always remember . . . your mother."*: AP, p. 23

CHAPTER 4: Young Chief Joseph
    PAGE 31 *"Our fathers were born . . . never leave them."*: AP, p. 21
    PAGE 32 *"A few more years."*: AP, p. 23
    PAGE 35 *"If there is any way . . . that it be done."*: HM, p. 134
    PAGE 37 *"superior nature."*: IP, p. 11
    PAGE 38 *"Joseph put his large black eyes . . . heart to me."*: IP, p. 21
    PAGE 39 *"Since my [friend's] life . . . than ever before."*: CG, p. 43
    PAGE 41 *"imperfect and incomplete."*: CG, p. 42
    PAGE 41 *"I think it a great mistake . . . valley for their own."*: IP, p. 23
    PAGE 43 *"When the white men . . . to live in peace."*: AP, p. 25
    PAGE 43 *"All I have to say . . . give up the land."*: CJ, p. 74

CHAPTER 5: Showing the Rifle
    PAGE 44 *"I did not want . . . hands of my people."*: AP, p. 43
    PAGES 45–46 *"Is he a chief . . . our country."*: CJ, p. 79
    PAGE 46 *"If we were to be massacred . . . than once."*: HM, p. 169
    PAGE 46 *"Who are you . . . what to do?"*: YW, pp. 39–40
    PAGE 46 *"I am that man."*: CJ, pp. 80–81
    PAGE 46 *"I am chief . . . what to do."*: CJ, pp. 80–81
    PAGE 47 *"All that hurt . . . showing us the rifle."*: YW, p. 41
    PAGE 48 *"The more [Indians] . . . the next war."*: GS
    PAGE 49 *"None of the chiefs . . . wanted war."*: YW, p. 42
    PAGE 49 *"If I had said nothing . . . against my men."*: AP, p. 37
    PAGE 50 *"I did not want . . . give up my country."*: AP, p. 43
    PAGE 50 *"Quiet peace reigns . . . every day."*: DR, p. 96
    PAGE 52 *"I would have given . . . by my people."*: AP, p. 51

CHAPTER 6: The War of 1877
PAGE 53 *"I had counseled peace . . . war would bring more."*: AP, p. 47
PAGE 56 *"You are getting fat . . . your scalps!"*: CJ, p. 102
PAGE 56 *"You cowardly people!"*: YW, p. 67
PAGE 58 *"Now, my people . . . ready for war."*: CJ, p. 241
PAGE 60 *"A lot of warriors . . . could not reach us."*: HM, pp. 317–318
PAGE 63 *"one of the worst . . . on this continent."*: DR, p. 137

CHAPTER 7: On the Trail to Montana
PAGE 64 *"We understood . . . the buffalo country."*: AP, p. 59
PAGE 68 *"Never shall I forget . . . have ever seen."*: BB, p. 27
PAGE 69 *"Their horses appear . . . and durable."*: LC, Feb. 15, 1806
PAGE 70 *"My shaking heart . . . buffalo country!"*: YW, p. 109
PAGE 70 *"My shaking heart . . . through this land!"*: YW, p. 109
PAGE 70 *"Looking Glass . . . by himself."*: YW, p. 11

CHAPTER 8: To Kill or Be Kind?
PAGE 72 *"We could have killed . . . cowardly an act."*: AP, p. 61
PAGE 73 *"I was half sleeping . . . what to do!"*. YW, p. 11
PAGE 73 *"Brave men . . . die fighting!"*: CJ, p. 260
PAGE 73 *"I would rather . . . fight!"*: CJ, p. 148
PAGE 77 *"These citizen . . . two tongues."*: YW, p. 130
PAGE 82 *"The squaws . . . watched me until morning."*: NP, p. 299
PAGE 83 *"They were treated . . . being insulted?"*: AP, p. 49
PAGE 84 *"I have my experiences . . . dead."*: CJ, p. 273

CHAPTER 9: Attack at Bear Paw
PAGE 85 *"With a prayer . . . I was not hurt."*: AP, p. 65
PAGE 86 *"Do not hurry! . . . all they want!"*: YW, p. 205
PAGE 87 *"You have seen hail . . . bullet hail."*: YW, p. 211
PAGE 88 *"With a prayer . . . I was not hurt."*: AP, p. 65
PAGE 88 *"Six of my men . . . twenty steps apart."*: AP, p. 67
PAGE 90 *"We dug the trenches . . . handy here [at Bear Paw]."*: HM, pp. 485–86
PAGE 92 *"That white flag was a lie!"*: YW, p. 215
PAGE 94 *"I do not wish . . . reddening the snow."*: CJ, p. 258
PAGE 94 *"sick and sad"*: HM, p. 498
PAGE 95 *"I am tired . . . fight no more forever."*: HM, p. 498
PAGE 95 *"From where the sun . . . fight no more forever."*: HM, p. 498

CHAPTER 10: Fame from Misfortune
PAGE 96 *"Let me be . . . act for myself."*: AP, p. 89
PAGE 96 *"No more battles . . . for good rest."*: YW, p. 224
PAGE 98 *"The chief . . . would carry out the order."*: AP, p. 75
PAGE 99 *"We gave up . . . our horses."*: AP, p. 75
PAGE 104 *"I want the white people . . . a man or not."*: AP, p. 3
PAGE 104 *"When will . . . tell the truth?"*: CJ, p. 313
PAGE 104 *"These Indians are . . . not be consulted."*: CJ, p. 325
PAGE 107 *"What I have to say . . . act for myself."*: AP, p. 89
PAGE 109 *"These Indians . . . in this locality . . ."*: CJ, p. 325

CHAPTER 11: A Broken Heart

PAGE 111 *"I have a kind . . . for all of you."*: CG, p. 336

PAGE 111 *"The places . . . I was alone."*: YW, p. 278

PAGE 113 *"I love that land . . . a wild animal."*: AP, p. 23

PAGE 115 *"Ever since the war . . . or anyone."*: SP

PAGES 115–116 *"I have a kind . . . for all of you."*: CG, p. 336

PAGE 117 *"Whenever the white man . . . one people."*: AP, p. 91

Image Credits

About the Author

Lorraine Jean Hopping is the author of the award-winning *Bone Detective: The Story of Forensic Anthropologist Diane France* and more than thirty other children's books. For titles and biographical information, visit her Web site at hoppingfun.com. She lives with her husband, Chris Egan, in Ann Arbor, Michigan.

Index

About Asleep, 60, 87, 117
Acquitted, 43, 118
Agents, government, 34
Baptized, 7, 118
Bear Crossing (wife), 71
Bear Paw
 cavalry charge, 86–88
 false truce, 91–93
 standoff, 88–91
 woman remembering, 90
Birth, of Joseph, 2–3
Boomtowns, 24, 118
Brothers and sisters, 7
Buck, Henry, 68
Bugler, 55, 118
Canada, 84, 86, 87, 88, 93,
 94, 96, 111, 117
Carpenter, Frank/Ida, 81, 82
Cavalry. See also Custer's Last
 Stand
 Bear Paw attack, 86–88
 defined, 118
 outrunning, 55–58
Childhood, of Joseph
 birth, 2–3
 boy and girl activities, 7–9
 as Chief's son, 9–11
 given Christian name, 3–7
 quiet, powerful presence in,
 14
Civil War, 25, 48
Clark, William, 6, 17, 59–61,
 69
Cody, Buffalo Bill, 112
Colville Reservation,
 108–110, 111, 113, 115,
 116–117
Commission, 41, 118
Continental Divide, 70, 118
Corps of Discovery, 6, 7, 69
Council of 1855, 15–22
Councils, chiefs and, 19
Cowan, Emma, 81, 82
Cradleboard, 58, 59, 118
Crow tribe, 61–62, 83, 99
Custer's Last Stand, 39, 40,
 77
Death, of Joseph, 117
Dreamer religion, 28–29, 46
Eagle from the Light, 36–37
Economic, 35, 118
Fame, of Joseph, 80–81,
 101–104

Fight no more forever speech,
 94–95
Findley, A. B., 38, 41, 43
Flathead tribe, 61–62, 66,
 83
Fort Keogh, 97, 98
Fort Leavenworth, journey
 to, 104–105
Fort Lincoln, journey to,
 98–100
Fort Missoula, 65–66
Frog
 death of, 88, 95
 Joseph and, as Chief's sons,
 9–11
 leadership of Joseph and,
 9–10, 14, 30, 31, 39, 42,
 50
 Nee-mee-pu name, 7
 photograph of, 42
 white murderers and,
 42–43
 wife killed, 75
Gibbon, Colonel John, 66,
 67, 75, 76, 77
Glossary, 118
Gold rush, 23–24
Grant, President Ulysses S.,
 34, 35–36, 38, 41
Grating Sound, Chief, 31–32,
 36–37, 45–47, 49, 52, 54,
 55, 61, 78, 84, 88, 91–92
Hair Combed Over Eyes, 58,
 70
Hair, Dreamer, 28, 29, 42
Hale, Calvin, 26–27
Hayes, President Rutherford,
 106–107
Homestead Act, 26–27
Horses
 loss of herd, 99
 Nez Perce, quality of, 68, 69
 riding hidden style, 9–10
Hot Place, move to, 105–106
Howard, General Oliver
 arresting Grating Sound,
 46–48
 council with non-treaty Nez
 Perce, 44–50
 demanding move to
 reservation, 43, 49–50
 Joseph saving, 49
 opinion of Joseph, 37–38

post-war comments on,
 115–116
supporting Nez Perce
 keeping land, 41
surrender to, 93–95
War of 1877 and, 53–54,
 55, 58, 59, 63, 64, 66, 75,
 76, 78
Innocent prisoners, 79–83
Land, of Nez Perce. See also
 Wallowa River valley
 agent for. See Monteith,
 John
 caution from dying chief on,
 30
 Dreamer religion and, 29
 fighting for, 62, 78, 115
 gold rush and, 23–24
 Howard advocating for, 41
 Joseph vowing to guard,
 32–33, 43
 moving to reservation from,
 50–51
 ownership controversy,
 32–38
 thief treaty, 26–27, 28, 32
 Treaty of 1855 and, 20–22
Lapwai mission, 3–7, 8–9, 12
Lapwai reservation, 43, 44,
 45, 49–50, 61, 93, 98,
 108, 111, 117
Lawyer, Archie, 33
Lawyer, Chief, 17–18, 21, 22,
 24, 27
Leadership, Joseph/Frog
 learning, 9–11, 14, 31
Lean Elk, 78, 79, 81, 82, 84,
 88, 102
Lewis, Meriwether, 6, 69,
 104. See also Corps of
 Discovery
Looking Glass, Chief, 21–22,
 32, 36, 37, 49, 50–51, 53,
 57–58, 61–63, 64–66, 70,
 77, 84–86, 89, 93, 95, 102
Mammoth Hot Springs, 83
McNall, Wells, 38, 41, 43
Migrants, 3, 56, 69, 105, 118
Miles, Colonel Nelson, 76,
 89–95, 96–99, 100,
 101–103, 104
Missions, 3–5, 8–9, 11–12,
 23, 118

Montana. *See also* Bear Paw
  Big Hole attack, 72–74,
    75–77, 78
  miserable retreat to, 61–63,
    64–65, 85
  resting in, 70–71
  safe passage in, 65–68
  Stevensville, 66–68, 77
Monteith, Frances, 46
Monteith, John, 33, 34,
  35–36, 38–39
Murder
  of white settlers, 11–12, 52
  of Wind Blowing, 38–43
Myths, facts and, 102
Native American,
  Indian/American Indian
  vs., 8
Nee-mee-pu ("the Real
  People"), 3, 4
Nez Perce. *See also* Land, of
  Nez Perce
  attacked, 1
  Corps of Discovery
    expedition and, 6, 7, 69
  councils and, 19
  meaning of, 4
  as *Nee-mee-pu* ("the Real
    People"), 3, 4
  non-treaty ("hostile
    Indians"), 28
  peaceful nature of, 5–7
  retreat of. *See* Bear Paw;
    Montana; War of 1877
  return to Northwest,
    108–110
  treaty ("friendly Indians"),
    28
Noise of Running Feet, 1, 87,
  108, 111
Old George and Captain
  John, 61, 92–93
Ott, Larry, 52
Peace
  at any cost, 49–51
  fight no more forever
    speech, 94–95
  as goal of Joseph, 9
  massacre teaching lesson of,
    12–13
Pierce, Elias, 23
Prophets, 29, 118
Ratify, 25, 118
Rawn, Captain Charles,
  65–66, 75, 76

Reservations
  annual report, 109
  defined, 118
  delaying move to, 49–50
  forcing Nez Perce to, 27
  Howard demanding move
    to, 42, 49–50
  moving to, 50–51
  refusal to move to, 43, 46–49
  today, 117
Reuben, James, 33, 35, 56,
  61, 108
Rifle, showing, 47–49
Roosevelt, President
  Theodore, 115
Scalp(ing), 39, 43, 78, 118
Seattle, final speech at, 116
Shaman, 45, 118
Sherman, General William T.,
  48, 62–63, 64, 75, 76, 89,
  104
Shore Crossing, 52, 70, 73
Sitting Bull, 39, 40, 41, 62,
  88, 111, 112, 117
So-ya-pu, defined, 4
Spalding, Henry and Eliza,
  3–5, 12, 28
Speaking with two tongues
  at Council of 1855, 20–22
  defined, 15
  gold rush and, 23
  white traders and, 77
Speech, famous, 94–95
Springtime (wife), 52, 58, 87,
  88
Stevens, Isaac
  background of, 15–16
  council with. *See* Council of
    1855
  speaking with two tongues,
    20–22
Telegraph, 75, 76, 79
Tepee poles, 9, 58–59, 64,
  70, 71, 74, 78
Tepees, 5, 7–8, 34, 60, 118
Thief treaty, 26–27, 28, 32
Thunder Rising Over Distant
  Mountains, 14, 109
Timeline of events, iv
Treaty
  of 1855, 22, 23, 25–26, 32,
    36, 41
  of 1863 (thief treaty), 27,
    32, 35, 41, 93
  defined, 118

Tu-eka-kas, Chief (father), 5,
  7, 12–13, 16, 18, 20,
  21–22, 27, 28, 30,
  112–113, 114
Vision quest, 13–14, 118
Wallowa River valley, 13–14,
  21, 22–23, 28, 30, 32–36,
  38, 41, 44, 78, 110,
  112–113
War of 1877. *See also* Bear
  Paw
  attack at Clearwater, 58–61
  food and supplies for,
    67–68, 78–79
  innocent prisoners and acts
    of kindness, 79–83
  Joseph taken prisoner,
    91–92
  long miserable retreat,
    61–63. *See also* Montana
  new chief in, 77–78
  outrunning cavalry, 55–58
  preparations for, 53–55
  relief after, 96–97
  revenge act leading to, 52
  start of, 54–55
  surrender, 94–95
  surrender talk, 84, 89–91,
    93–94
  teenager's view of, 60
  telegraph and, 75, 76, 79
  Wayakin name, 14
White Bird, Chief, 31, 36–37,
  49, 50, 53–54, 55, 62, 67,
  70, 73, 78, 84, 89, 93, 94,
  96, 98, 117
White settlers
  gold rush and, 23–24
  Homestead Act and, 26–27
  murders of, 11–12, 52
Whitman massacre, 11–12,
  18
Whitman, Perrin, 45, 46
Williams, Mark, 33
Wind Blowing, murder of,
  38–43
Wives, of Joseph, 1, 31, 52,
  71, 117
Yellowstone Park, 79–83
Yellow Wolf, 47, 49, 54–55,
  58, 70, 73, 77, 80–81, 87,
  92, 94, 111

Discover interesting personalities
in the Sterling Biographies® series:

Muhammad Ali: *King of the Ring*

Marian Anderson: *A Voice Uplifted*

Neil Armstrong: *One Giant Leap for Mankind*

Alexander Graham Bell: *Giving Voice to the World*

Cleopatra: *Egypt's Last and Greatest Queen*

Christopher Columbus: *The Voyage That Changed the World*

Jacques Cousteau: *A Life Under the Sea*

Davy Crockett: *Frontier Legend*

Marie Curie: *Mother of Modern Physics*

Frederick Douglass: *Rising Up from Slavery*

Amelia Earhart: *A Life in Flight*

Thomas Edison: *The Man Who Lit Up the World*

Albert Einstein: *The Miracle Mind*

Anne Frank: *Hidden Hope*

Benjamin Franklin: *Revolutionary Inventor*

Lou Gehrig: *Iron Horse of Baseball*

Geronimo: *Apache Renegade*

Matthew Henson: *The Quest for the North Pole*

Harry Houdini: *Death-Defying Showman*

Thomas Jefferson: *Architect of Freedom*

Joan of Arc: *Heavenly Warrior*

Chief Joseph: *The Voice for Peace*

Helen Keller: *Courage in Darkness*

John F. Kennedy: *Voice of Hope*

Martin Luther King, Jr.: *A Dream of Hope*

Lewis & Clark: *Blazing a Trail West*

Abraham Lincoln: *From Pioneer to President*

Jesse Owens: *Gold Medal Hero*

Rosa Parks: *Courageous Citizen*

Pocahontas: *A Life in Two Worlds*

Jackie Robinson: *Champion for Equality*

Eleanor Roosevelt: *A Courageous Spirit*

Franklin Delano Roosevelt: *A National Hero*

Babe Ruth: *Legendary Slugger*

Sacagawea: *Crossing the Continent with Lewis & Clark*

Sitting Bull: *Great Sioux Hero*

Tecumseh: *Shooting Star of the Shawnee*

Jim Thorpe: *An Athlete for the Ages*

Harriet Tubman: *Leading the Way to Freedom*

George Washington: *An American Life*

The Wright Brothers: *First in Flight*

Malcolm X: *A Revolutionary Voice*